Innovate Your
Innovation Process
100 Proven Tools

Innovate Your
Innovation Process
100 Proven Tools

Shlomo Maital

Technion-Israel Institute of Technology, Israel

NEW JERSEY · LONDON · SINGAPORE · BEIJING · SHANGHAI · HONG KONG · TAIPEI · CHENNAI · TOKYO

Published by

World Scientific Publishing Co. Pte. Ltd.

5 Toh Tuck Link, Singapore 596224

USA office: 27 Warren Street, Suite 401-402, Hackensack, NJ 07601

UK office: 57 Shelton Street, Covent Garden, London WC2H 9HE

British Library Cataloguing-in-Publication Data

A catalogue record for this book is available from the British Library.

Cover image and text illustrations courtesy: Avi Katz (www.avikatz.net)

INNOVATE YOUR INNOVATION PROCESS
100 Proven Tools

ISBN 978-981-4759-94-6

Desk Editor: Sandhya Venkatesh

Typeset by Stallion Press
Email: enquiries@stallionpress.com

Printed in Singapore

Introduction

In today's fiercely competitive global marketplace, organizations large and small increasingly endure and prevail through their innovativeness. Nearly every organization has well-run well-organized processes for production, marketing, quality control, accounting and human resource management. Yet many organizations, especially smaller ones, lack such a well-defined process for innovation — one that is precisely aligned with the organization's values, products and personality. It is essential to understand that an R&D department is *not* a full-blown innovation eco-system that enlists creative thinking throughout the organization, starting with the mail room and maintenance crew. Instead, an R&D department can wrongly signal that creative ideas are 'quarantined', coming only from those within it, even though those in R&D are often in least contact with the clients.

This book provides over 100 concise innovation tools, proven ones, usually accompanied by mini-case studies or stories showing how each were applied. The learning objective for readers is to understand these tools and then construct a personalized, detailed systematic process for generating creative ways for creating value, for products, services and processes that is perfectly in tune with the organization, its history and its clients and workers.

A productive innovation process is unique to every organization, just like a fingerprint is unique for each of nearly 8 billion people on earth, with 80 billion fingerprints, and is assembled like a puzzle in creative ways using both what other organizations have learned, as they innovate, and out-of-the-box thinking that assembles the innovation process pieces in new and unique ways. If one essential piece is missing, the puzzle is incomplete.

The mantra of this book is: Entrepreneur, Global Manager — innovate how you and your organization innovate. When you succeed, you will generate not just one great innovation, but an endless stream of them. I hope the 100-plus tools described in this book will prove productive, interesting and helpful.

Innovation paradoxes: The innovation process, like the creative process that drives it, is fraught with many internal contradictions. The term 'innovation process' itself is almost an oxymoron — while innovation demands open, often wild, creative ideas, implementing those ideas requires a smooth, organized, disciplined system, the antithesis of the ambience that generates new thinking. Yet without a disciplined innovation process, creative ideas never advance beyond sketches on scraps of paper.

The creative process is often built on two contradictory ideas, both of which cannot be true. This creates what psychologists term "cognitive dissonance" — major discomfort in our thought processes. Many people try hard to resolve such dissonances quickly, often by adopting one or the other of the two conflicting ideas. But creative people have been shown by research to be very good at holding conflicting ideas in their minds for very long periods, ultimately integrating them to produce some idea that is entirely new.[1] Readers will quickly find that some of the stories in this book contradict others. For instance: Innovate in teams; innovate in pairs; innovate as a creative individual. All three are true. Which works best for *you? For your organization?* Are you part of Lennon and McCartney (the Beatles)? Part of Apple's amazing design team? Or a lone-wolf innovator, spinning off ideas and products from your fertile brain?

---

[1] See, for instance, Roger Martin, *How Creative People Think*, Harvard Business Review, June 2007. Martin quotes F. Scott Fitzgerald, the American novelist: "More than 60 years ago, F. Scott Fitzgerald saw "the ability to hold two opposing ideas in mind at the same time and still retain the ability to function" as the sign of a truly intelligent individual."

Innovation Paradoxes: There are at least six innovation paradoxes, drawn to my attention by a colleague, Prof. Ella Miron-Spektor.

* Passion vs. Profit: Innovation is driven by passion, as its rocket fuel. But if you focus solely on passion, ignore the hard reality of profit, you cannot build a sustained business. How to resolve?
* Huge hairy challenges vs. build self-confidence: Innovation builds on huge hairy challenges. But, frequent failure ruins self-confidence, the key resource of creative people.
* Personal empowerment, initiative, vs. shared goals: Ideas come from individuals, who are highly motivated. Yet delivery of ideas is done by teams, who need shared goals, where the individual personality is submerged.
* Diversity vs. cohesion. Diverse teams work best. Yet cohesion is vital for delivery of ideas.
* Learn from history vs. detach from the past. You need to learn from the past. But you also need to forget the past, in order to create the future.
* Incremental vs. radical innovation: you need to make small improvements to existing things; but you also need to reinvent entire product categories or industries.

Innovator: How can YOU resolve these paradoxes? Find a creative way to do so, and make it a key part of your innovation process. Above all — be aware these paradoxes exist, have to be managed, and have to be somehow resolved, without destroying either of the key two propositions. The astute reader will find many of these paradoxes in the 100-plus stories in this book. But in the end, each innovative person will have to resolve them, in their own way.

This book is not a textbook. It contains no checklists, how-to lists, or 2x2 box diagrams. It is comprised solely of stories. Yet the subtitle claims that the book provides 'tools'. *How can stories possibly be tools?*

The answer is, stories are among the most powerful tools for learning. We learn from the stories of others. And we learn by creating our own stories. Psychologists use stories to heal, in narrative therapy; family doctors use narrative medicine in a similar fashion.[2] In each story in this book, an

---

[2] "Narrative therapy is a form of psychotherapy that seeks to help people identify their values and the skills and knowledge they have to live these values, so they can effectively confront whatever problems they face" (*Source*: Wikipedia).

inspired innovator has made use of a creative method, approach, idea or system to implement innovation and change the world.

I invite my readers to write their *own* story. Create a narrative, in which you are the central figure, the protagonist. How did you come upon an idea? What did you do to implement it? Who used it? Whose lives were changed by it? How did it make people happy? How did you follow up on your initial idea, with an unending stream of new ideas? How did you become a serial innovator that changed the world? Write your own narrative — and then, most important, act to make it come true. It is fun to dream, but dreams change the world only when they are made to come true by determined, hard-working individuals. Creativity is a happy merger of ideas that are both novel and useful. And useful implies that someone actually makes use of the idea, for their betterment.

I have resisted the temptation to spoon-feed the reader by summarizing each tool, in each story. This is part of the learning process — read the story, and ask yourself, what can I use here, adapting it to my needs, personality, values and creative thinking? *How can I make this proven approach part of my own innovation process? How can I innovate the way that I myself, and my organization, innovate? What can I take home from this story?*

A narrative is defined as a series of connected events. The connections are usually teleological, or causative, A causes B causes C. The "C", in the stories in this book, is usually a creative idea, implemented creatively. The 'tool' in the story is the causal links between A, B and the result, C.

In one sense, the stories are all the same. A is the germ of an original idea. B is the steps taken to implement it. And C is the result. But the A to B to C teleology takes an enormous variety of forms, and in each, the narration comprises a possible tool that can help innovators, after it is understood, processed and adapted to individual needs.

All the stories in this book were written for my innovation blog, found at *www.timnovate.wordpress.com*. I wrote the first blog on April 21, 2007, and since then I have written more than 1,300, a pace of about two blogs a week. It occurred to me that I could organize the blogs around different themes and publish them as a book that hopefully will be helpful for innovators. I'm grateful to World Scientific for making it possible to do this. I continue to add new blogs nearly every day. For me, my blog is part of the creative process. When you know you need to find new ideas to write about, it keeps your scanning radar and brain active all the time. Once you turn on your "personal innovation machine", you will never want to turn it off, even when the innovation process itself can be difficult, and fraught with pain and struggle.

A final word. Albert Einstein defined creativity as "intelligence having fun". I like this definition, even though research has shown that creativity and intelligence are not correlated. (Intelligence is knowing old stuff; creativity is inventing new stuff. There is no obvious link between the two). Innovation is at once very hard, involving long hours and hard work, pain from continual failures, ridicule, opposition, mocking, humiliation, and cynical responses — and a great deal of fun, far more than doing the same thing over and over, as many of us may be doomed to do.

Have fun. Innovate. Change the world. I hope some of the stories in this book will help you do so.

I invite readers to share their thoughts, ideas and experiences with me, by email: smaital@mit.edu.

Shlomo Maital
Haifa, December 2015

Contents

For innovators, everywhere, whose ideas bring peace
and happiness to a troubled world

CHAPTER ONE

Stories That Inspire About People Who Aspire

Introduction

Research has shown that the single variable most closely correlated with creativity, by far, is motivation.[1] Creative people are highly motivated to come up with new thinking, to tackle tough problems and meet unsatisfied wants. Motivation comes from within. But sometimes, creativity can be sparked by a story of another person, who changed the world through innovation. I'd like to do that, we think. I *can* do that. At least I can try.

The stories in this chapter are designed to inspire. They all about ordinary people who do extraordinary things. I believe everyone can. And even if this is not the case, "everyone can!" is a very good, productive working hypothesis. These are stories that inspire, about people who aspire — and take action!

---

[1]See A. Ruttenberg & S. Maital, *Cracking the Creativity Code*, SAGE (India), 2014, p. 105.

What we learn from Ivo Karlovic's 156 mph serve!

If you like tennis, and perhaps even if you don't, you can learn a lot from a Croatian pro tennis player named Ivo Karlovic.

Karlovic was a 15-year-old teenager living in Zagreb, Yugoslavia, during its bitter civil war. He practiced his tennis daily at the Salata tennis club, but could find no-one to play with him. (Tennis balls hurt when they hit you, but bullets hurt a lot more.)

So he gathered 200 balls and practiced his serves, for hours, imitating his role model, the Croatian pro Goran Ivanisevic. He would serve 200 times, go to the opposite court, and serve again 200 times … to no-one.

Ivanisevic holds the world record for "aces" (serves that win a point outright, without being returned), at 10,183. Karlovic is getting close. He has 10,004 aces and will soon break the record.

Karlovic is 6 feet 11 inches tall, the tallest pro player on the tennis circuit. His serve comes from 11 feet high, screams across the net at speeds averaging 132 mph, and is clocked at times at 156 mph. So — try hitting that! His big serve enables him to win 96 percent of his service games. And though he's in his mid 30's, he is getting better, rising in the pro ranks.

What can we learn from Ivo? Leverage your advantages — in this case his height. Accept your constraints (practicing during civil war) and overcome them. Make the best of what you have. Practice hard. Make no excuses. And aspire to excel.[2]

---

[2] *Source*:   http://www.nytimes.com/2015/08/13/sports/tennis/ivo-karlovic-king-of-aces-closes-in-on-a-record.html

Innovation lessons from the sports page: Go, Katie Ledecky!

What can you learn about creativity and innovation from the *New York Times* Sports Page?

It turns out, a lot.

Karen Crouse has written about Katie Ledecky, American swimmer competing in the world championships in Kazan, Russia. She did an amazing feat. She swam in the 1500 meters final, and broke the world record. In fact, she SMASHED the world record, by 2.23 seconds! She swam 30 laps, 1500 meters, in 15 minutes, 25.48 seconds. About one minute per 100 meters.

And then?

Only one hour later, she got back in the pool … and swam in the semifinals for the 200 meters freestyle. And somehow, qualified for the final.[3] This, despite fatigue.

Nobody has ever done that before or even dreamed of trying it.

What's her secret?

"I wasn't afraid to fail," she said, adding, "I had nothing to lose."

And, digging a bit deeper: Here is how Crouse explains it:

Ledecky is the way she is partly because of a combination of her mental toughness and the unconditional love of her inner circle. Ledecky's parents, Mary Gen and Dave, dispense hugs, not technical advice, leaving the post race analysis to Ledecky's coaches. They support her swimming but do not smother her with expectations. Their view is that whatever she accomplishes in the water is but one strand in a rich life tapestry that includes academics and service and family.

---

[3] See http://www.nytimes.com/2015/08/10/sports/rethinking-an-olympic-format-in-light-of-katie-ledeckys-1500-feat.html

There you have it. Mental toughness. And the unconditional love of her inner circle. The right to fail. And the unconditional love that remains, win or lose.

Our kids are inspired to do great things when we raise the bar high, give them high aspirations, support them … but always, stressing that failure is often inevitable and thus is not a problem. Go for it, if you fail, we're here, we love you, always will, we love you for who you are and not for the medals you win.

Go, Katie! We've learned a lot from you. Thanks.

Meet John Osher: What we learn from SpinPop & SpinBrush

As a retired Technion professor with silver hair and lots of stories, I get to meet and greet many visitors. Yesterday I had lunch with one of the most interesting ones — an American entrepreneur named John Osher. Here is his story.

Osher grew up in Ohio; he took 7 years to finish college. He worked as a plumber, carpenter and cabdriver. He was an entrepreneur from age 5, he tells me. He started and sold a vintage clothing store, and an earring outlet, while still in college. Harvard Business School Professor William Sahlman, who wrote a lengthy case about Osher, says, "he's a street-smart guy and he has this observational power. He hated having to manage employees, so he built a big company with very few employees."[4]

Dr. John's was Osher's third major venture built from the ground up and ending in a lucrative exit. He produced the uniquely American (and 'insanely popular') SpinPop battery-powered lollipop, which later led to SpinBrush. SpinPop is a lollipop that spins in your mouth (using a tiny battery-powered motor), enhancing the flavor, and creating a new market category of "interactive candy". In developing the product, Osher focused

---

[4]See   http://hbswk.hbs.edu/item/from-spinpop-to-spinbrush-entrepreneurial-lessons-from-john-osher

laser-like on cost, setting cost targets and determining that if they were not met, the product would not be produced.

I teach, "don't fall in love too soon with your product", I told Osher.

Osher answered: NEVER! Never fall in love with your product. Easy to say, hard to do, when dedicated entrepreneurs bring immense passion to their endeavors.

After SpinPop's success, Osher simply walked up and down the aisles of Wal-Mart, and looked for product ideas that could build on the cheap-battery/electric-motor technology of SpinPop. He came up with 100 of them. Then he narrowed them down to an inexpensive electric toothbrush, to become SpinBrush. Here was his plan: Produce an electric toothbrush that would have a battery life of at least 3 months, and cost only $1.49 to manufacture! Sell it retail at $5.00.

I told him that what he did fit two of our models, in our book Cracking the Creativity Code. First, zoom in, zoom out. Zoom in on "SpinPop" and what you learned from it; Zoom out to find ideas that can leverage it. Then Zoom in again, to implement the idea. Second, Price Cost Value. Start with high value (e.g. electric toothbrushes that create value, because people are willing to pay $50 for a Braun). Make it at very very low cost. Then charge a reasonable price, to share the value between profit margin (for the company, price minus cost) and client margin (for the buyer, value minus price). (You get, say, a $50 electric toothbrush for $5 — that's value!)

Osher is very modest, quiet-spoken, and very very wealthy — he sold SpinBrush to Procter & Gamble for nearly half a billion dollars. He achieved this with soaring head in the clouds imagination (Lollipops that spin???? Give me a break!) and hard-nosed, hard-headed, feet-on-the-ground pragmatism.

Anyone can do this. All you need is imagination, experience, objectivity, pragmatism, leadership, drive, energy, hard work, and persistence.

Thanks, John, for showing the way.

Cool Idea? What else can you do with it?

As described above, entrepreneur John Osher invented a lollipop that spins in your mouth, created a huge hit, and then, tireless, asked, what else can I do with a cheap tiny electric motor that spins things? His answer was: an inexpensive electric toothbrush. Result: a half billion dollar (acquisition by Procter & Gamble).

Here is another example. Elon Musk succeeded against all odds in building and selling Tesla electric cars. His cars are cool, beautiful, fast, expensive, green and in demand. They are not hybrids. They run solely on electric power. The core technology is the rechargeable electric car battery.

Like Osher, Musk asked, what else can I do with what I know about batteries that store electricity? Answer — build batteries that can store solar power, so that at night, when the sun doesn't shine, you can still have power. Storage is a crucial element to the success of solar power, because people consume electricity not only in daylight but also at night. And so far, the storage element is missing.

According to Diane Cardwell, writing in the *International New York Times*,[5] Tesla Motors is initiating a "fleet of battery systems aimed at home-owners, businesses and utilities". One of the products will be a lithium ion rechargeable battery pack, four feet by three feet that can be mounted on a home garage wall. The battery will be called the Powerwall, and will sell for $3,500. It was derived from the car batteries that power the Model S vehicles.

The proposed batteries will be connected to the Internet and can be managed by Tesla from afar.

The key to this idea? Tesla is building a $5 billion battery production plant, called the Gigafactory, in Reno, Nevada.

This story reminds me of the 9-word capsule description of successful entrepreneurship. First to imagine (Musk did). First to move (Musk did). And first to scale (Musk is). And, add to that — first to platform (take one good product and transform it into another).

---

[5] See http://www.nytimes.com/2015/05/01/business/energy-environment/with-new-factory-tesla-ventures-into-solar-power-storage-for-home-and-business.html

Starbucks & Howard Schultz: He's for real

Is Howard Schultz for real? Are his pro-social activities and investments genuine? Or is it all an act, to promote Starbucks?

Writing in the *New York Times*, columnist Joe Nocera answers: He's for real. Schultz grew up poor in Canarsie, Brooklyn, housing projects, bought a small coffee chain in Seattle and turned it into Starbucks, global giant coffee shop chain employing 23,000 with annual sales of $16.5 billion. He was CEO until 2000; when he turned over management to someone else, Starbucks quickly crashed, and Schultz returned to the CEO job in 2008. Starbucks' market value rose from $5.3 billion at the time, to today's $92.3 billion (as of November 30, 2015). Clearly, Schultz knows something about managing and growing businesses.

But what Nocera particularly stresses is Schultz's social vision. Here are some of his projects:

- In 2011, he called for a boycott on political contributions, until the two parties Democrat and Republican began to work together.
- He began a project to make loans to small businesses, partly with money from the Starbucks Foundation, when the economy was struggling.
- He co-authored a book about the plight of American military veterans, and donated $30 million to this cause from his family's foundation.
- He has launched a medical company, with Rajiv Chandrasekaran, that will use storytelling to tackle important social issues.
- He started, last month, Starbucks' Race Together campaign … including 10 forums for Starbucks' employees to discuss race issues.
- He has promised to hire 10,000 youths who are neither in school nor in the work force.
- He will open Starbucks stores in disadvantaged neighborhoods, including Ferguson, Mo.

Schultz's vision is to re-establish the American Dream, which he himself lived. As one scholar pointed out, it is not just the inequality in wealth and income that is disturbing, in America, but the lack of social mobility, the ability to move from lower deciles to upper ones, as Schultz did. The American Dream has become the American Myth. Schultz wants to rebuild it.

Personally, I think Starbucks coffee is … well, in my view, not very tasty. It is Robusta, rather than Arabica, because Robusta is cheaper — half the price of Arabica green beans. But let's give Schultz credit. He knows how to manage, and he also has a highly pro-active conscience. We need more Howard Schultzs.

Anthony Ray Hinton: 28 Years on death row: What he teaches us all

The *BBC World Service* reports: "A man released from prison after nearly 30 years on death row in Alabama has blamed his conviction on being black and poor. Prosecutors dropped the case against Anthony Ray Hinton, 58, when new ballistics tests contradicted the only evidence that linked him to the murders of two restaurant managers in 1985."

The man is Anthony Ray Hinton. And he has every reason to be bitter, angry and disconsolate. Society took away his life, unjustly. Three decades on death row, the term for prisoners awaiting capital punishment, is almost unimaginable torture — cruel and unusual punishment, banned by the Eighth Amendment to the U.S. Constitution.

So, how does he really feel? And how did he retain his sanity, while on death row for 28 years, beginning when he was only 29 years old? (He is twice that age today.) The *BBC* reports: "Asked if he felt angry about the people who imprisoned him he said: "I am a joyful person. I have a good sense of humor and that's what kept me for the 30 years I was locked up. *I couldn't let them steal what I had left which was joy. They had robbed me of my 30s, my 40s and my 50s so if I get mad and hate them I'm letting them steal my joy."* He said he was taking life "one step at a time" and wanted to "just try to live within my own means, *try to bring joy to someone else, live a fruitful life and just be happy".*

I believe that if Anthony Hinton can still seek to "bring joy to someone else", after nearly 3 decades on death row, surely all of us can do the same!

And by the way — we learn one more thing from Hinton's release, according to his lawyer: "Mr Hinton is the 152nd person to be exonerated after being sentenced to death. It's a shocking rate of error. No system would tolerate that rate of error that cared about the people that were at risk but because most of the people on death row are poor or people of color we seem to not care as much that some of them are innocent."

Larry Page: As innovator role model

Fortune magazine chose Larry Page as Business Person of the Year.[6] The feature article begins with a revealing joke, told often around Google. At Google's "moon shot" Google X center, where self-driven cars, high-altitude wind turbines, and stratospheric balloons for Internet access are developed, a 'brainiac' creates a time machine. As the scientist reaches for the power cord to start a demo for Larry Page, Page says: "Hey! Why do you need to plug it in!?"

For a decade Page was one member of a triangle — Sergei Brin, Eric Schmidt, and Page — that led Google. In 2011 Page took over as CEO. Turns out he is a good manager. In the past three years, Google has grown 20 percent annually, and has quarterly revenue of $16 billion. It has $62 billion in cash. Page invests heavily both in Google's core business (he says he argued with Steve Jobs, who said, 'you guys are doing too much') and in far-flung new projects. According to *Fortune*, in the past year, Google has invested in artificial intelligence, robotics and delivery drones. It has

---

[6]http://fortune.com/businessperson-of-the-year/

expanded its venture unit, which invests in startups and is a kind of scouting team. It bought Nest, a smart-home startup. It invested in Calico, a biotech firm.

Originally Google set out to "organize the world's information and make it universally useful and accessible". Today that vision is too narrow. Page says he wants Google to change the world in ways most of us cannot imagine.

Some say Google is too narrowly focused on advertising revenue. But YouTube now brings in $6 billion in annual revenues. Page continues to invest in bold ventures, to ensure the company's future. He is making 'credible bets' on the home, the car, and wearable devices.

Most amazingly, Google has a secret facility where a team of scientists are working on a project that will chemically 'paint' tiny nanoparticles, with a protein, so they bind to things like cancer cells. And then concentrate them through magnetized wearable devices, so they can be 'queried'. This would enable constant monitoring and detection of a whole host of devices. Outside Google's core competence? Not at all.

Page regards some of his bold bets as a portfolio bucket. Some will pay off. Many won't. He doesn't think the risk is high. By the time you want to put large sums of money into something, you pretty much know whether it will be profitable, he says. For him, not taking risks is the biggest risk of all.

Marathon man: 365 marathons, 365 days!

Stefan Engels is a Belgian runner, from Ghent who had a crazy idea — to get people interested in running, rather than "sitting in front of the TV with a bag of crisps (potato chips)". He would do it by a dramatic *Guinness Book of Records* feat — run one marathon a day, EVERY day, every single day, rain or shine, for a whole year, 365 days.

And despite injury, exhaustion, diarrhea (in Mexico) and other problems, he succeeded. It was a tremendous triumph of will power. Once,

Stefan had to do the marathon with a hand-cycle, because his legs were injured. But mostly, he ran, and once in a while, walked.

Let's do the numbers. In all, over a year, he ran 9,563 miles or 15,330 kilometers. His usual pace was four hours, or 6.5 miles per hour (10.5 kilometers per hour).

Stefan is bandy-legged — his legs turn inward. This should have led to serious injury, as the stress went up his legs into his back. But in general it did not. He runs very economically, with low leg lift, and very light footfall.

A documentary about him, *Marathon Man*, tells the story.

For those of us who have done one or two marathons in their lifetime, running one a day for a year is mind-boggling. Stefan — we salute you. Anything is possible, indeed.

Jeanie Leung: Follow your passion!

As I write this, my wife and I are in Hong Kong, at Hong Kong University of Science and Technology, a truly great research university where I will give five lectures. HKUST is only 23 years old, founded in 1993, yet it is now ranked among the world's top engineering and science universities, owing to clever innovative leadership.

My friend Amylia took me on a tour of HKUST yesterday and by chance, in the library, we stumbled on an exhibition by an artist Jeanie Leung. (See her website: www.jeanieleung.com, and 'like' her on Facebook, Jeanie Leung.) Jeanie is an HKUST graduate with a BBA (Bachelor's in Business Administration). She worked successfully in banking. But her passion was art, even though she has never formally studied painting.

One day, she quit her job, left the secure paycheck — and set out on an adventure. She wrote a series of wonderful books, child-like in quality but with powerful serious messages, illustrated by her incredible acrylic-on-paper paintings. The series of four books is called *Colours of Stories*. Yesterday I met her in person at her exhibition and got her autograph.

Jeanie typifies two key principles. One is: Follow your passion! She has, and has been eminently successful. The second is: Discovery and Delivery, you need both. She had a brilliant concept for her books. But she works exceptionally hard to implement them. She finishes a painting in 2–3 days, and it takes over 40 of them to make a book. From a video, it appears she works on the floor. HKUST is helping her market her books and is giving her moral support — despite her abandoning the business world for the world of art and books.

Congratulations, Jeanie. I hope others will follow your example.

Too small to see? A Nobel for three who pioneered

The 2014 Nobel Prize for chemistry was won by two Americans and a German: Eric Betzig, Stefan Hell and William Moerner. Their work greatly extended our vision into the smallest of molecules, in part enabling nanotechnology.

Hell, born in Romania, heads the Max Planck Institute in Gottingen, Germany. Moerner is from Stanford University; and Betzig, from the Howard Hughes Institute in Virginia.

According to *CNN*: "Back in 1873, science believed it had reached a limit in how much more of a detailed picture a microscope could provide. At the time, microscopist Ernst Abbe said the maximum resolution had been attained."[7] As with so many Nobel Prizes, the three winners simply did not accept the statement, "we've reached the limit — no more can be done."

The three scientists, according to the Nobel Prize Committee, did this: " … Due to their achievements, the optical microscope can now peer into the nanoworld," the committee said. "The importance can't be overemphasized: Now, scientists can see how proteins in fertilized eggs divide into embryos, or they can track proteins involved in Alzheimer's or Parkinson's diseases."

Betzig and Moerner found a way to make single molecules 'glow' using fluorescent microscopy. Hell found a way to use two laser beams to

---

[7]http://edition.cnn.com/2014/10/08/world/europe/nobel-prize-chemistry/

make the molecules glow. This is creative thinking. Rather than conventionally illuminate molecules with photons, why not make the molecules themselves into little 'lamps'?

"Guesswork has turned into hard facts and obscurity has turned into clarity," the Nobel Committee added. The work of the three has "blurred the boundary between chemistry and biology", by enabling us to see right inside single molecules.

Thank you, scientists!

Alexandra Scott & the $80 million lemonade stand

The next time you think about tackling a hard problem you really care about, but hesitate because the odds are long — I hope you'll remember this story.

Alexandra "Alex" Scott was born in Connecticut in 1996. Before she turned one year old, she was diagnosed with infant neuroblastoma, a type of childhood cancer that attacks nerve cells and is hard to treat.

In 2000, just after turning 4 years old, she informed her mother she wanted to start a lemonade stand to raise money for doctors to "help other kids, like they helped me."

Her first lemonade stand raised $2,000. It led to Alex's Lemonade Stand Foundation. Alex continued her lemonade stands project throughout her life, and eventually she raised over $1 million toward cancer research!

Alex lost her fight. She died in August 2004; she was only 8. Today, Alex's Lemonade Stand sponsors a national fundraising weekend every June called *Lemonade Days*.

Each year, 10,000 volunteers at more than 2,000 Alex's Lemonade Stands around the nation make a difference for children with cancer. Some $80 million has been raised so far.

Life gave Alex lemons … and she literally made lemonade, giving new meaning to that old cliché.[8]

---

[8] http://www.mnn.com/lifestyle/responsible-living/photos/8-amazing-kids-who-have-changed-the-world/alexandra-alex-scott#ixzz393snZiwD

But that isn't art! Jeff Koons triumphs

American artist Jeff Koons, who is 59, has at last been accorded a full-career survey show in a U.S. art museum, at the Whitney Museum of American Art, which has had to empty most of its exhibits to accommodate Koons' work. I was fortunate to view the exhibit and found it fascinating.

Who is Jeff Koons and what can we learn from him about innovation? First, think different. Koons makes art out of ordinary objects. One of his sculptures is a set of four Hoover vacuum cleaners, in a plastic case. But that's not art, many will say. Well, it is, if you're willing to open your mind to rule-breaking art.

You may not believe this, but last November Koons achieved a record auction price for a living artist when someone paid $58.4 million at a Christie's auction in Manhattan for Balloon Dog (Orange). It's 10 feet high (over 3 meters), made of stainless steel. When the press mentions the $58.4 million price, Koons says (according to TIME magazine): "as a young artist I wanted to be engaged in the excitement of making art and sharing ideas. And that hasn't changed — that's what the art world represents to me."

It is what innovation and creativity represent as well — the excitement of making art and sharing ideas. Creativity in any field is (or should be) "autotelic", a word meaning, self-generating, self-causing, from "telos", Greek for cause, and auto, self.

Koons father owned a furniture store in York, Pa., an industrial city that lost its industry. There, Koons learned about the power of ordinary objects to become art. One of his famous sculptures is a basketball, in a blue-glass aquarium; the ball floats precisely in the middle of the tank, because Koons found just the right combination of distilled water and salt water to make that happen. In general, he is a stickler for detail. He has a team of 130 people in his art studio who produce works of art according to Koons' specification. His studio even invented its own steel alloy.

As you can imagine, Koons was ridiculed early in his career. He stuck to his guns. He went broke several times, to pay for the huge cost of preparing his sculptures precisely as he wished. Koons says he has had very few exhibitions in the United States, although he is known and popular abroad. Perhaps, as he turns 60, his own country will at last recognize his work and creativity.

Ibaka: Mental toughness trumps genius

Serge Ibaka is a star player for the Oklahoma Thunder, a leading basketball team in the U.S. NBA (National Basketball Association), a team that battled San Antonio Spurs for the Western Conference championship and the right to play Miami Heat in the NBA finals. Ibaka is from the Republic of Congo, and a citizen of Congo and Spain.

Ibaka was injured. He could barely walk. His team was down two games to none to San Antonio and on the verge of being eliminated. So Sunday, he decided to play. Oklahoma won 105-92, with Ibaka, a stellar defender who leads the league in blocks, playing a key role. (He is 6′ 10″, 245 lbs., won a silver medal with Spain in Olympic basketball 2012, and gold in the European Championship in 2011.) Oklahoma is a different team when he plays. Star players Kevin Durant and Russell Westbrook score scads of points, but Ibaka is vital for keeping the opponent from scoring.

Why did he play while injured? Ibaka grew up very poor. His family suffered during the Second Congo War; his father was imprisoned. He played basketball on concrete, with worn out shoes or no shoes. He moved to France, then to Spain, playing with second division clubs and working his way up. He was one of 18 or 20 children. His mother died when he was 8. Then civil war broke out in Congo.

Here is what he said, when asked why he played injured. ″The military, when they go out there to fight, when they sign up, they sign for everything. No matter what happened last night, I signed up for this.

That's what I get paid for. When we sign here in the NBA, we sign on everything, man."

Ibaka was in superb physical condition when he was injured. This is in part why he could come back so quickly. He is known as a rim protector, and is given nicknames like *Air Congo*, *Serge Protector* and *iblocka* by his teammates.

Ibaka teaches us that mental toughness, commitment, loyalty, persistence, resilience, and in general character trump genius and innate skills. He has a $12 million contract with Oklahoma. It hasn't spoiled him. Because for him, it's not about the money.

Ibaka reminds me of Fred Smith, founder of Fedex. Smith invested $48 million to launch Fedex. When asked whether he was not fearful of losing the money, he explained that he had served in Vietnam as a Marine, was in life-threatening situations, and "when you can lose your life, losing money has no fear."

Ibaka knew real hardship. Playing hurt, playing through pain, was not even close.

Nicholas Negroponte: Where do ideas come from?

MIT Prof. Nicholas Negroponte was the featured speaker at the 20th anniversary event of the MIT Enterprise Forum of Israel, an organization I helped found in 1994, and now run by Ayla Matalon. Negroponte spoke about how and why he started the Media Lab, together with MIT President Jerome Wiesner. His plan was to create a place for outsiders, for those whose radical innovative ideas would never be accepted in conventional MIT faculties.

"Where do new ideas come from?" Negroponte asked the audience, rhetorically. In one word: "From differences." From people who think differently.

I think this explains why so few really new ideas emerge from universities, places where creativity is supposed to live but never does, and from big corporations, which pay lip service to innovation but do everything to stamp it out.

Universities reproduce ideas, by having students do research that in tiny incremental steps extends the research of their advisors, and generally affirms it. Imagine a thesis that disproved the central theories of the advisor! Tenure is gained fastest and easiest by publishing mainstream research that irritates no-one and ruffles the fewest feathers.

Businesses grow to global scale by operational discipline, in which people are well paid to do the same thing, again and again, with excellence and discipline. Imagine a manager who tells his CEO that the company's most profitable product line is becoming commoditized and should be sold or closed.

Neither universities nor large multinationals want their people to think differently. Nor do they hire people who are different. This, despite the well-known finding that it is the most diverse teams that are the most innovative, and the rule that you should include a non-expert in every team, to ask the 'dumb' questions.

I strongly urge my students to respond to job interviews with their own interviews. Interview the interviewer. Find out if they really do want your creative ideas. Find out if they celebrate failure, and welcome diversity. Do this before you get put into the corporate blender and emerge as bland conventional porridge, instead of remaining a spicy jalapeño pepper.

From basic biological science to market success: How Bob Langer changes the world

Bob Langer is a renowned MIT scientist. His famous lab has generated an endless stream of inventions that benefit mankind, including radical new methods for controlled-release drug delivery. This is important — when we swallow a pill, the concentration of the drug in our blood rises, then falls, then rises again when we take another. Controlled-release technology keeps the level of the drug constant, in our blood stream, so that it is more effective.

Prof. Langer shared his "secret of success" in a recent article in *Nature Biotechnology*, a leading scientific journal.[9] It includes 3 "P's": platform, paper, patent.

* Platform: develop a technology that can be used over and over in different applications and technologies. For instance, his method for controlled release drug delivery systems also found use in microspheres for food applications, e.g. fat substitutes.
* Paper: Publish your results in a high profile journal; "peer review validates the idea". You must of course file for a patent within a year of publishing the paper.
* Patent: "ideally, file a blocking patent, that protects the platform, and all the ways it can be used and applied".

Platform, paper and patent — all persuade investors of the validity of the idea. Add to this two more P's: P of P, proof of principle — show the technology is viable. Speed is vital, adds Langer; the more rapidly you can get to clinical trials, the better. And you need a champion. Langer's champions are his doctoral students, who develop technologies in their Ph.D. theses, then go on to found companies. Langer often serves on the board, makes introductions, helps get financing. Langer himself is a bench scientist, and focuses exclusively on scientific research. But his vision has led to many many spin-off companies emerging from his lab. At a time when many biotech startups fail, Langer appears to have developed a winning formula. If I were in biotech, I would study the Langer Lab formula closely.

Gifts from the gifted: Richard Branson (Virgin)

I just finished writing a magazine column about a gifted young woman who is 27. She has a Ph.D., is married, created software that can predict the

---

future, has a black belt in karate, won a coveted prize, interned at Microsoft, did Army service, and is now launching a startup. Interviewing her led me to reflect how many wonderful gifts humanity receives from such gifted people. But what is special about them?

I came across a study of a very gifted entrepreneur, Richard Branson, of Virgin fame (I counted over 40 Virgin companies, ranging from travel agencies to music to mobile to...everything; the name 'Virgin' happened because Branson and partners felt they were 'virgins' in business when they started their first company). The study is by Larisa V. Shavinina, of the University of Quebec.[10] Branson is the 6th richest individual in Britain. She lists the causes of Branson's entrepreneurial giftedness. Here are just a few:

* "rule breaking": I always enjoyed breaking the rules, Branson says; e.g. 'no 17-year-old can edit a national magazine', so he chose to do so.
* "initiative": He broke rules to do things better, not just to rebel. At school, he wrote the headmaster, making concrete suggestions regarding school meals, etc.
* "create value": I never went into business purely to make money. A business has to exercise your creative instincts.
* "fierce independence": I never enjoyed being accountable to anyone else or not in control of my own destiny, he notes.
* "love of challenges and adventure": Balloon flights and the Virgin companies form a seamless series of challenges I can date from my childhood, he writes.

Shavinina notes that Branson's parents supported his entrepreneurial instincts strongly, and his grandmother holds two British records: Oldest person to hit a hole in one in golf (90), and oldest to pass the advanced Latin-American ballroom-dancing examination. 'You've got one go in life," she told Branson, "so make the most of it." He listened. Branson's Aunt Joyce lent him the money to set up his music company, when he was 20, when the banks refused. His Aunt Clare was an entrepreneur who built a business on an endangered species of Welsh Mountain sheep. Clare flew a biplane and liked to parachute. Branson named his first child after her.

---

[10] Larisa V. Shavinina, *Early Development of Entrepreneurial Giftedness*, ASAC Administrative Sciences Association of Canada, 2007.

Amar Bose, 1929–2013

We can all learn many things from Amar Bose, founder of the speaker and earphone company, who just passed away at the age of 84.

1. In a 2004 interview with *Popular Science,* he said: "I would have been fired a hundred times at a company run by M.B.A.'s. But I never went into business to make money. I went into *business so that I could do interesting things that hadn't been done before.*"
2. Build the change you seek. Dr. Bose (he held 3 degrees from M.I.T.) was disappointed by the bad sound of a costly stereo system he bought when he was an M.I.T. engineering student in the 1950s. He realized 80 percent of the sound in a concert hall bounced off walls and ceilings before reaching the audience. This was the basis of his research. In the early 1960s, Dr. Bose invented a new type of stereo speaker based on psychoacoustics, the study of sound perception: many small speakers aimed at the surrounding walls, rather than directly at the listener. In 1964, his mentor at M.I.T., Dr. Y. W. Lee, urged him to found his company, The Bose Corporation.
3. Persist! His first speakers fell short of expectations, but Dr. Bose kept at it. In 1968, he introduced the Bose 901 Direct/Reflecting speaker system, which became a best seller for more than 25 years and made Bose a leader in a highly competitive audio components marketplace; the 901s used a blend of direct and reflected sound. Later Bose Wave radio and the Bose noise-canceling headphones became market and technological leaders.
4. Give back. Dr. Bose had a passion for teaching. He returned from a Fulbright scholarship in New Delhi and joined the M.I.T. faculty in 1956. He taught there for more than 45 years. In 2011, he donated a majority of his company's shares to the school. (Bose never 'went public', in order not to lose control of his company's direction.) The gift provides M.I.T. with annual cash dividends. M.I.T. cannot sell the shares. Bose got a lot from MIT — mainly its culture that drives graduates to start businesses. And he gave back a lot too.

Becoming Jack Dorsey — and why you should

Jack Dorsey, born in St. Louis, is 36 years old. He is the founder of Twitter, which has changed the way the world communicates. How? Here is his story, as told to the CBS program *60 Minutes*.

As a child, Dorsey had a speech impediment and partly as a result was extremely shy. He found solace in computers, and taught himself to program before he was 12. He dreamed of working in New York City and got a job with a package delivery firm there by hacking their website, then offering to show them how to fix it.

In St. Louis, he amused himself by listening to 911 emergency dispatchers on a police frequency scanner. He noticed that all their messages were very short. Who am I? Where am I? What am I doing? Where am I going? Seven years ago, he launched Twitter on that basis — simple, short messages. So that everyone in the world "who owns a $5 cell phone could communicate with the world" — how I feel, what I'm doing, where I'm going.

Dorsey understands that technology should disappear. It should be so simple for users that they are unaware of it. This principle is usually forgotten — look at how complex it is, for instance, to set up a home router — something I've been struggling with. He was awarded by *The Wall St. Journal* the "Technology Inventor of the Year" award.

Dorsey was kicked out of Twitter by other founders and the Board of Directors. He calls it "a punch in the gut". Like Jobs, also kicked out of Apple, later, he was invited back. He says he does not bear a grudge. Meanwhile he has founded another path breaking company that is changing the world, called Square. Plug a dongle (white square) into the earphone plug, and you have a way to start a business and accept payment. The idea came from his friend Jim McAlvy, a nerd and artist, who lost a sale of a piece of art because he could not accept a credit card. Square is now used by many small businesses and has $12 billion turnover yearly. When you enter, say, a café, the iPad of the owner identifies you instantly (through GPS), your face appears on the screen, and two touches charge you for the coffee and send you a receipt. Simple. Transparent. Easy.

Dorsey is highly self aware. He knows his faults. Here is how he describes them: "I like to think about things myself. And then come out with a decision. I can be silent at times, this unsettles people. Biggest thing I've learned, I need to communicate more, be more vocal."

At Square, he has no office or even a desk. Everything is on his iPad. He walks around and constantly talks to the workers.

He once considered running for Mayor of New York, to replace Michael Bloomberg, who recently completed his final term of office.

If I could, I'd have voted for him.

Why should we become like Jack Dorsey? And how? Honesty. Transparency. Simplicity. Self-awareness. And modesty. And superb marshaling of creativity to tackle unmet social needs. One person can indeed change the world, hugely — and more than once.

Sara Blakely hated how her butt looks — and made a billion!

On February 21, 2015, Sarah Blakely celebrated her 44th birthday. Who is Sara Blakely? She is the youngest woman (an American) to reach *Forbes'* "billionaire" list, self-made, on her own, without husband or family wealth. She is 416th on the *Forbes'* billionaire list.

How did she do it? By making something she personally needed and wanted and did not exist. Innovation can be very personal. Here is her story.

She was working as a sales trainer by day and stand-up comedian by night. She knew zero about pantyhose (except, she hated them), and had never taken a business class. "I had only one source to operate from ... my gut", she says.

She hated the way her fanny looked, wearing regular panties. She decided to do something about it; because she was sure many other women felt the same way. She developed a fanny-scrunching panty using Spandex, wrote the patent herself and it was approved. Then she trade-marked the name SPANX. For months she drove around North Carolina begging mill owners to manufacture her product. Finally, after many rejections, she found a mill owner who agreed. Why? Because, he said, he himself had two daughters.

It took a year to perfect the prototype, because Sara was obsessed that her Spanx should be comfortable. (After all — she would wear them herself.) She chose the Spanx name carefully, and it proved to be a winner. ("It's edgy, fun, catchy, and makes your mind wander," she says, "and it's all about making women's butts better, so why not?")

She took a bold new approach to packaging — if your product is innovative, its package has to look it — and chose a bold red package with three women on the front. She called the buyer at Neiman Marcus, a top-of-the-line department store chain. She agreed to give Sara 10 minutes. Together, they went to the ladies' room, and Sara showed the buyer her butt, in her cream pants, before Spanx … and after! Three weeks later Spanx was on the shelves of Neiman Marcus. She did the same with Saks, Nordstrom, Bloomingdales and others. She asked her friends to go to the stores and make a huge fuss over her product.

She had no money to advertise, so she hit the road. She did in-store rallies about Spanx with the sales associates, and then stayed all day introducing customers to Spanx. And she got help from media women; her product was on the *Oprah Winfrey* show, for instance, and on *Tyra Banks' Show*. To get free publicity for Spanx, she even joined Richard Branson's reality show *The Rebel Billionaire*, leaving her business for three months to do daring tasks all over the world.

Sara has now launched a foundation, to empower women all over the world. She summarizes: "My energy and inspiration come from inventing and enhancing products that promote comfort and confidence for women. Customer feedback is one of the key drivers of our business."

How many millions of women looked in the mirror, turned around, and did not like what they saw below the waist? One bold woman did something about it. And now she's a billionaire. Annual revenues are $250 million and her net margin is estimated at 20 percent.

And she started with the modest sum of $5,000 in personal savings.

Good work, Sara! Innovation really is personal.

Make meaning: When tragedy becomes triumph

On February 6, 2010, tragedy struck a family from central Israel, hiking in the snow in the Golan Heights. The rare snowfall obscured signs warning of land mines. As a result, one of the three children in the family stepped on a mine. "We threw snowballs and played around for five minutes," 11-year-old Daniel Yuval said. "Then I remember taking a step forward and I heard the explosion. For a few minutes I don't remember much. My father picked me up." Daniel's leg had been severed by a landmine. There were some 260,000 more landmines in the area.

Daniel is a tough, brave kid. Within a month he walked his first steps. He allowed his dressings to be changed, painfully, without painkiller. And he quickly made up the time he lost in school. After his leg was blown off, he asked his father Guy (who was carefully retracing his steps with Daniel in his arms, to avoid other mines) to stop and re-attach his lost leg.

Daniel wrote a letter to all 120 members of Israel's Parliament, and launched a high-profile campaign to clean up land mines. He spoke to Parliament, to the Foreign Affairs and Defense Committee. A bill is now being promoted, costing $89.4 million, to clean up the land mines.

According to anti-mine campaigner Jerry White, founder of the anti-landmine organization Survivor Corps (White himself lost his leg while hiking in the Golan), "Daniel Yuval is the tipping point where Israelis woke up."

If an 11-year-old can overcome losing his leg, and find meaning in the incident, to work to keep others from the same fate, surely the rest of us can find meaning in far less painful circumstances.

"When I awoke from the surgery at the hospital and saw my amputated right leg," he wrote in his letter to Israel's Knesset members, "I told my mum that I wanted no one else to ever be hurt by a landmine, and that I meant to do something about that." And he did.

Transforming adversity and depression into meaning is often simply about acting, rather than complaining. Daniel Yuval did. We can all learn from him. And Daniel? He follows artificial limb technology closely and still dreams of playing football (soccer), his main passion.

Benjamin Franklin, Innovator: Back of the bus, da Vinci!

On a long flight, recently, I read Benjamin Franklin's Autobiography on my Kindle. I realized that while we attribute multidisciplinary creativity to da Vinci, in art, science, engineering, urban planning, etc., when it comes to practical needs-based innovation driven by a deep understanding of society, the Boston-born American innovator Benjamin Franklin (1709–1790) is far ahead.

Franklin was born and raised in Boston, on Milk St., but left at an early age to find his fortune. He was self-educated and read widely. Here are a few of his innovations, driven by an independent inquiring mind:

He invented the lightning rod (flying a kite into an electrical storm that by all odds should have electrocuted him), the Franklin stove (highly efficient stove), bifocals (he wore them), the urinary catheter (none of his inventions were patented; he utterly opposed such wealth-creating monopolies). He wrote, "as we enjoy great advantages from the inventions of others, we should be glad of an opportunity to serve others by any invention of ours; and this we should do freely and generously". He charted and named the Gulf Stream Ocean current. Once doubting sea captains believed him, they cut two weeks off the voyage between North America and England. He founded the *American Philosophical Society*, where scholars could present their research findings. He first noted that electricity has positive and negative charges. Franklin published ideas for sea anchors, catamaran hulls, watertight compartments, shipboard lightning rods and a soup bowl designed to stay stable in stormy weather. He founded the University of Pennsylvania. He invented the public library. He innovated the post office and stamps. He realized there was a shortage of printed money and, against the wishes of the wealthy oligarchs who controlled what little currency there was, printed currency to foster commerce. To this day the Franklin Mint prints currency and mints coins, in Philadelphia.

And finally, Franklin helped write that amazing document, the *American Declaration of Independence*.

The fundamental difference between Leonardo da Vinci and Benjamin Franklin was that da Vinci tried to keep his innovations secret by his mirror-writing, and most of them were thus never implemented. Franklin, in contrast, purposely sought to give away his ideas and implement them as rapidly and as widely as possible. Generally he succeeded. His method was one widely taught today: Identify a social need, build a business model to acquire resources (he liked to use a subscription model — pay a small regular fee and enjoy library services, or hospital, or education, or postal services).

It is worth re-reading his Autobiography; innovators will find much in it to emulate.

Shirley Temple: From Good Ship Lollipop! To diplomacy

Shirley Temple Black passed away on February 10. She was 85. She became famous when she began a movie career when only 3 years old, and in 1935, when she was only 7, won a special Academy Award for her movies. As a child star, she once made 8 movies in a single year. During the Great Depression her movies brought joy and relief to millions. Shirley Temple's signature song was *On the Good Ship Lollipop*, which sold 500,000 sheet music copies.

Child movie stars often have troubled adolescence and adult lives. But Shirley Temple figured it out. She realized that her ringlets and precocious acting, singing and dancing would evaporate when she grew older. After an unhappy first marriage, she married Charles Black and became a diplomat, serving the United States in the United Nations and as Ambassador to Ghana and Czechoslovakia.

When asked what her secret was, she said, with a smile: Start early.

The *BBC* recounts a great Shirley Temple story. She was once invited to The White House to meet President Roosevelt and his wife Eleanor. When the First Lady was bending over, Shirley (who was a tomboy) pulled a slingshot out of her pocket and fired a stone at the First Lady's rear end.

Eleanor Roosevelt stood up with a start. The Secret Service scoured the room ... but no one suspected the curly-haired little angel.

Shirley Temple's life shows us that most of us, perhaps all of us, will need to reinvent ourselves and our careers at least once, when our skills and capabilities are made irrelevant by the rapid pace of change. We can do as Shirley did, and simply move on, adapt, adjust and find something new, or we can wallow in bitterness and regret. Like Shirley Temple, each of us needs to think well in advance, what will I do next, when what I do now is no longer relevant? Increasingly, this question of "when I become irrelevant" is increasingly relevant.

And it's best to start now. Innovation is also about careers. It is also about how we remain useful, relevant value-creators for our entire lives, by constantly seeking to become, ourselves, novel. As Gandhi urged: Become the change you seek.

CHAPTER TWO

From Ideas to Action

Introduction

Death Valley, between California and Nevada, got its name in 1849 during the California Gold Rush, when 13 prospectors died crossing it in a wagon train on their way to the gold fields. It has the world's highest recorded temperature, 134 degrees F. (57 degrees C.), and average yearly rainfall of only two inches (5 centimeters). Crossing Death Valley is perilous.

There is a metaphorical Death Valley between having an idea and implementing it. Most ideas perish, between the moment they appear in our brains, and the time they are actually put into practice and are used by ourselves and by other people. According to Gary Hamel, and his negative exponent law, commercially successful ideas, X, equals about $2 \times Y \times 10^{-3}$, where Y is the number of original creative ideas. Ideas perish, because having ideas is fun and often easy (though not for everyone), while making them happen, by gathering together people, teams,

29

resources and systems, is very hard. One or two out of a thousand ideas endure and prevail.

The stories in this chapter are all about how to implement ideas. How do you take your tiny germ of an idea, and grow it into a huge tree offering shade, fruit, and pleasure for the masses? It is often believed that Leonardo da Vinci was history's most creative individual. True, he had incredible ideas, centuries before their time — the airplane, tank, submarine, parachute, and many more. But he built none of these. He simply wrote in his diary in backward 'mirror' writing. He didn't wish others to know about them, because many of his inventions were war machines (that's what he was paid for, by the city-state feudal rules of the time) and he had no desire to kill people. So, was da Vinci truly creative? In the realm of ideas, of course. In the realm of implemented ideas, probably not. Novelty? Unparalleled. Useful? Not very, because few of his ideas were put into practice.

For some, it is enough to dream. For others, it is insufficient. The test of a dream is its impact. These stories are about dreamers who knew how to make their dreams happen.

Five life lessons: Learning life forward

The great Danish philosopher Soren Kirkegaard once defined the tragedy of life: "We live life [looking] forward, we learn life [looking] backward". My wife and I visited York University, in Toronto, Canada, where I spoke to a class of young engineers, just beginning their studies, at the invitation of my host, Prof. Andrew Maxwell, who heads the BEST Bergeron Entrepreneurship for Science & Technology program in the Lassonde School of Engineering. I shared with them these five life lessons that I have learned personally:

1. Take on BIG challenges: challenge yourself hugely. If you fail, failure is glorious, and you learn a lot, so much that there really is no such thing as failure, when you're tackling something enormous. If you succeed — well, your life takes on huge meaning.

2. Start with WHY! Find something you are deeply passionate about. This will be your rocket fuel. Start with this, and move on from this point. Many of my young students do not yet know what their life passion is, because no-one has asked them, nor have they asked themselves. Use your passion to fuel your rocket — but first, be sure to find such a passion. Nietzsche once said that if you have a powerful 'why' (reason, meaning, or motivator), you can endure the most terrible 'how'.

3. Be like da Vinci: in SOME ways. Leonard da Vinci was immensely creative, he invented the submarine, tank, airplane, parachute, and vastly more things. He drew left-handed in his notebook, and wrote notes in mirror writing, to keep them secret. So in this — be UNLIKE him. Don't keep secrets. If you never share your ideas, you'll never improve or find people to help you implement them. But of course, share with people whom you trust.

4. Be truly expert in at least one thing, go deeply into it; and learn a little about everything you can, you never know. Steve Jobs studied calligraphy (handwriting) at Reed College. Why? It interested him. Because he did, the Macintosh, when launched, had beautiful fonts. This led to desktop publishing. Desktop publishing saved the Mac, created a huge market, and it was utterly unintended … simply because Jobs loved beautiful fonts.

5. Become very comfortable with being uncomfortable. All great things emerge from people who are uncomfortable about something — they just HATE it, can't tolerate it, want to CHANGE it. Much of modern life is about becoming, and remaining, comfortable, free of thirst, hunger, pain, boredom, anything uncomfortable. So get uncomfortable about something, and be comfortable with it, because THIS is what will drive you to action.

How to be an evangelist: From Guy Kawasaki

Guy Kawasaki was the legendary marketing guru for the Macintosh computer. Apple hired him, even though he was in the jewellery business at the time, had a psychology degree from Stanford, and knew next to nothing about personal computers.

Why did Apple hire him? Because — he believed. He felt that MS-DOS, and Microsoft in general, were "crimes against humanity". He felt that "Bill Gates brought darkness to the world." He set out "to right a wrong". He was in his words — an evangelist.

The Greek roots of the word evangelist mean "one who brings or proclaims good news". The word has come to mean someone who preaches the Christian gospels.

Kawasaki became a venture capitalist (garage.com), and now is Chief Evangelist for Canva, a startup whose mission is to democratize design. In the latest issue of Harvard Business Review, Kawasaki sets out the rules for becoming an evangelist. Here they are:

1. Schmooz. Build social connections. It's easier to evangelize people you know.
2. Get out of your cubicle. Network. Talk to people.
3. Ask questions. Initiate a conversation, then — shut up and listen.
4. Follow up. Make sure that you follow up on a meeting, within a day.
5. E-mail effectively: Optimize your subject lines, and shorten your text. Always respond quickly.
6. Make it easy to get in touch.
7. Do favors. If you do things for others, they are more receptive to listen to you.
8. Public speaking: An evangelist must master the art of public speaking. Kawasaki says it took him 20 years to master the art and get comfortable.
9. Deliver quality content. 80 percent of the battle is having something worthwhile, interesting, perhaps novel, certainly meaningful, to say. It is NOT just about how you say it, but what you say.
10. Omit the sales pitch. If people think you are pitching, you're dead. Don't.
11. Customize. Use the first few minutes to directly address the audience, show them you've done your homework, and know who they are and what they seek.
12. Focus on entertaining. If people are entertained, they are more receptive to the information you bring.
13. Tell stories. Make it personal. Tell stories about yourself and others that support your message.
14. Circulate in the audience beforehand. Make contact with them, especially with those in the front rows.

15. Control what you can. Try to speak at the beginning of an event; choose a small room, if you can. A packed room is better than a half-empty one.
16. Practice. You need to give a speech 20 times to get good at it.

Kawasaki adds several rules specific to social media innovation:

17. Offer value. Share good stuff — of four kinds: information, analysis, assistance, entertainment.
18. Be interesting.
19. Take chances. Don't be afraid to take strong stands, express feelings.
20. Keep it brief.
21. Be a mensch.
22. Add drama.
23. Tempt with headlines. How to … Top 10, etc.
24. Use hashtags.
25. Stay active: 3–20 different posts a day.

He concludes: "Evangelism is not about self-promotion. It's about sharing the best of what you, your team and your organization produce with others who can benefit."

Reinventing the automobile: GM & Ford vs. Startup Guy

"In the ring, weighing in at about four ounces, is Silicon Valley startup guy Paul Elio. Facing him, weighing in at 24,382 tons, is … General Motors, Ford, and VW. 12 rounds for the innovation championship in motor cars."

No contest? A startup to make cars? Non-starter, right? Well, Paul Elio has done it. There is a long long waiting list to buy the Elio automobile, a 3-wheeler that gets 84 miles per gallon! This beats even the hybrids! The car is American made! And its cost? $6,800. (About the cost of 2½ high-end Armani backpacks.) Here is what the Elio website says:

"A few short years ago, automotive enthusiast Paul Elio sized up the prevailing status quo of personal transportation. He saw the soaring costs of the vehicles we drive. He saw fuel prices spike to record highs almost daily. He saw Americans struggling with an economy that was taking too much and giving back too little. Paul Elio decided that the world was ready for something radically new. The result? A three-wheeled master-piece of automotive brilliance that bears his name." Elio's vision? "To pro-vide a fun-to-drive, super-economical personal transportation alternative, that's affordable, safe, and environmentally friendly. We are committed to the American dream, creating American jobs, and bringing American automotive ingenuity to every vehicle we build. This is, and will remain our mission at Elio."

The boxing match has begun. It ends as soon as it begins. Elio knocks out the automobile giants. Why? Big companies cannot innovate. By defi-nition. They would never let a car like the Elio get past the drawing board. Low profit margins, etc.

Elio Motors might yet fail. But like Tesla, it could spur the car compa-nies to actually try something innovative. Innovation comes from rebels. And rebellion is the last thing big companies seek or even allow.

Kudos to Paul Elio! And Big Oil? Think about trying another business.

Entrepreneur — Go work for government! Really!

The last place entrepreneurs think about, as an employer, is government. Government is too slow, wasteful, doesn't work, bureaucratic. Right?

Harvard Business School Senior Lecturer Mitchell B. Weiss disagrees. He is offering a Harvard course on Public Entrepreneurship. He knows what he is talking about. He worked as chief of staff to the late Boston mayor Thomas Menino, a great mayor. He co-founded the Mayor's Office of New Urban Mechanics, which invented America's first big-city 311 app, in which citizens alert governments to potholes and graffiti.

Harvard's online magazine *Working Knowledge* claims that cities around the world have increasingly become laboratories in innovation, partnering with outside businesses and nonprofits to solve thorny public policy problems. State and local governments, too, are trying this.[1]

---

[1]http://hbswk.hbs.edu/item/why-entrepreneurs-should-go-work-for-government

Weiss says one reason we don't have innovative people in government is because "we weren't training them. In public policy schools we were not training young people to be entrepreneurial, and at business schools we were not prepping or prodding people to enter the public sector or even just to invent for the public realm."

He notes that governments should be naturals at crowdsourcing — who has a bigger crowd than government, essentially, everyone?

Weiss says, "in government we announce something and wait to get it perfect. By using more experimental approaches, some public leaders are achieving success by testing and learning, instead of writing a plan in stone before executing it."

The Mayor of Jerusalem, Nir Barkat, is a former entrepreneur, founder of a successful startup BRM that made and sold early antivirus software. The former Mayor of New York City Michael Bloomberg is a highly successful entrepreneur who founded the company named after him. Both are, and were, highly creative in their terms of office.

Weiss says there is a huge opportunity in public entrepreneurship. Note that this is not social entrepreneurship. It is taking on operational roles in government, and bringing to the job creative ideas to make people's lives better. Why should creativity live and thrive only in the private sector, or in launching a not-for-profit social enterprise? Why not in government itself?

The Daniel Arm: Act! Don't Just Fret!

In our new book *Cracking the Creativity Code*,[2] the first of 10 key principles for structured creativity is this: 'Act, Don't Just Gripe'. Take action to right a wrong, rather than just talk about it — at least some of the time.

Writing in *The Guardian*, Emma Bryce recounts how Mike Ebeling, a Los Angeles resident and entrepreneur, did just this.[3]

---

[2]Arie Ruttenberg & Shlomo Maital. *Cracking the Creativity Code: Zoom in/Zoom Out for More Fun, Creativity & Success.* SAGE (India), 2014.

[3]http://www.theguardian.com/lifeandstyle/2014/jan/19/3d-printer-bomb-victim-new-arm-prosthetic-limb

He is the founder of an American startup called 'Not Impossible Labs', an organization that builds open-access devices to assist people facing seemingly insurmountable physical challenges, Ebeling recounts how *TIME* magazine wrote about Daniel Omar, South Sudan, who in March 2012, at the age of 14, "embraced a tree trunk to shield himself from a bomb's blow, and stepped away without his hands. Aware of the burden he would place on his family, in 2012 Omar told a *TIME* reporter that he would rather have died when the government's Antonov aircraft dropped its lethal cargo." [This brings to mind the current Syrian Government's policy of dropping oil drums filled with explosives on civilian buildings in Aleppo and elsewhere, killing thousands].

Seeing this declaration on paper shocked Mick Ebeling. Ebeling read this and thought, "I've got three little boys... it was hard for me to read a story about a young boy who had lost his arms." Repeatedly, innovation is very personal, because it is driven by motivation, and motivation is often most powerful when it matters most to the innovators themselves.

Here is what he did, according to Bryce. "In November 2013, Ebeling travelled to Sudan for a month, hoping to find Daniel and build him an arm. He took with him printers, spools of plastic and cables. The 3D printers that create the prosthetic's plastic parts make the device seem hi-tech, but the resulting arm is really just a simple, mechanical device. The arm works by using movement to trigger cables, threaded throughout the plastic structure like ligaments. When the user flexes and bends the remaining portion of their arm, this motion tenses the cables, which in turn curl and uncurl the fingers at the tip."

"Since Ebeling has returned home, one prosthetic a week has been printed, thanks to two 3D printers he left behind. The machines sit humming industriously — mostly at night when it's cool enough for them to work. The printed parts are then collected by eight local people trained to operate the machines, assemble the arms, and customize them for recipients."

Ebeling identified an unmet need, one he was passionate about; thought creatively about simple, inexpensive solutions (the prosthetic arm costs a total of $100, a fraction of conventional prosthetics), and took action, getting on a plane and going to the site.

If only more of us would do the same.

Superheroes: Meet the 3D printer prosthetic hand

The preceding story was about Daniel Omar, South Sudan, and his 3D prosthetic arm, created by an American startup called 'Not Impossible Labs', founded by Mike Ebeling. Ebeling found a way to create inexpensive functional prosthetic arms for Sudanese children badly wounded in the Sudanese Civil War, by using 3D printers and teaching locals how to use them to 'print' arms.

The New York Times carried a story, "Making the Hand of a Super Hero", by Jacqueline Mroz, which reports that another online volunteer group, E-nable, founded by Dr. Jon Schull, "matches [American] children in need of prosthetic hands and fingers with volunteers able to make them on 3D printers."[4] Designs are downloaded onto the machines at no charge. Charity indeed begins at home. These prosthetic limbs cost as little as $20 to $30, a fraction of the cost of conventional prosthetics, and they work just as well.

And the neatest part? The limbs are designed to look like, say, limbs from 'Transformers' or cyborg superheroes. A photo shows 'Cyborg Beast', a prosthetic hand that could well be one used by superhero Steve Austin, the bionic man. Rather than try to hide or disguise them, they are in bright fluorescent colors and scream, 'hey look at me! I'm cool!' The prosthetic hands say, I'm not disabled, I'm actually, well, kind of a superhero. And "transformer" is the right word — the printed hands transform a disability into a superhero cool device.

Some of the statistics that demonstrate need are shocking. Some 9,000 American kids suffer amputations yearly just as a result of lawn mower accidents alone and one in 1,000 infants is born with missing fingers.

We're still waiting for 3D printing to change our lives. Meanwhile, good people have discovered a wonderful use for them. As always, the best ideas are always the simplest.

---

[4]http://www.nytimes.com/2015/02/17/science/hand-of-a-superhero.html

What polite people say when they say bathroom: How gleaming bathrooms built an innovation

How do you say "bathroom", if you're very polite, delicate, and discreet and don't actually want to use the 'b'-word? In Britain, you could say, I'm going to spend a penny, because that's what it once cost to use a public toilet. Today it will cost you 30 pence... is that inflation, or what? Or you could say, I need to go to the loo … or the WC (Water Closet). Or, I'm going to powder my nose, if you are female. Or, I'm going to the little girl's room … The list is endless.

But bathrooms are serious! Here is a story I heard, from a very senior academician, in Kaunas, Lithuania, where my wife and I attended a school psychology conference.

Many years ago, universities were launched to enroll young Lithuanian men who sought to avoid military service. [Lithuania was the first Soviet satellite to gain its independence, in March 1990; other countries like Poland quickly followed suit. The USSR sent troops, but they gave up and finally left in 1993].

Someone had a brilliant idea that young Lithuanian women too wanted and needed to go to college, and started a college for women only. He suffered ridicule ("Geisha University", and worse), but persevered. Faculty were brought from outside Lithuania, many of them women.

How do you attract, and keep senior female faculty, in Lithuania, at a time when it was relatively poor? Where do you invest your resources?

Bathrooms, under the Soviets, were utterly disastrous. And let's be honest, bathrooms matter to women especially, because of, well, anatomical issues. I've known women to suffer in order to wait to get to a clean decent bathroom.

So, this innovative Dean invested his resources in — gleaming beautiful lovely modern bathrooms. And it mattered. It was the first thing visiting female faculty noticed. A very small detail, but a crucial one. He had the most beautiful bathrooms in Lithuania. And by doing so, communicated to his visitors that he understood them and would do everything to make their stay pleasant.

God is in the details, especially when it comes to innovation. Keep this in mind the next time you visit an unworthy bathroom.

Let the sunshine in!

"Somewhere, inside something there is a rush of Greatness, who knows what stands in front of our lives, Let the sunshine, let the sunshine in, The sunshine in, Let the sunshine, let the sunshine in, the sunshine in ..."[5]

Those are the words of a song from the musical 'Hair'. According to Suzanne Daley, writing in *The New York Times*, a small Norwegian factory town, Rjukan, has taken those words seriously. Rjukan is nestled in the Norwegian mountains and once was the site of the world's first modern fertilizer factory, in 1906. Because of its northerly location, and because of the mountains, for six months of the year Rjukan residents do not see the sun — at all. The sun rises and sets quickly, and never gets high enough to rise over the surrounding mountains. But they've found a solution that made this little town famous all over the world.

Three huge solar-powered and wind-powered mirrors move in concert with the sun, and focus a beam of sunlight on the town square. Thousands of people come to the square, wearing sunglasses and carrying beach chairs. Suddenly the town became more social. After church on Sunday, people flock to the square, enjoy the sunshine and converse and chat.

"It's been a great contribution to life here," said Annette Oien.

What can we all learn from Rjukan? I am blessed to live in a country, Israel, with sunshine nearly every day, often strong sunshine. One philosopher even claimed that three great religions were born in the Middle East because of that strong sun, whose powerful stark shadows of dark and

---

[5]http://www.metrolyrics.com/let-the-sunshine-in-lyrics-hair.html

light remind us of the sharp contrast between good and bad, right and wrong.

But even here, in bright sunlight, there is much darkness. People who are ill, lonely, depressed, who live in poverty.

Can we learn from the people of Rjukan, and MAKE sunlight, in our own lives and in the lives of others — where there is only darkness? It's not that hard. A smile, a kind word, some encouragement, a pat on the shoulder … It's worth a try. We innovators *can* let the sunshine in.

How to fix America's health care problems: Experiment!

President Barack Obama: I apologize. I criticized you fiercely for incompetence, for the inability to even set up a simple website for your 'Affordable Care' legislation. Sorry. Turns out it wasn't so simple. Reforming health care, within a completely broken existing system, is tough. You now have 7 million people signed up for 'ObamaCare'. This is a big achievement.

But it's only a start. America still spends 18 percent of its GDP on health care, a vastly inflated sum, with little to show (life expectancy is below that of countries that spend less than half that).

In *The New York Times*, Molly Worthen describes an experiment in Vermont ('Live Free!' is the state's motto), the state of independent-minded voters. It's called 'Green Mountain Care'.[6] The idea came from a third party, the Vermont Progressive Party. It's a single-payer system, which regulates doctor's fees (translation: keeps doctors from inflating them) and covers all Vermonters' medical bills. The system could spread to other states.

This is how to resolve social problems. Let each of the 51 American states try its own system. Check which of them work and then replicate them across America.

How do I know this works? It worked in Canada. I grew up in Regina Saskatchewan. In 1959 Premier Tommy Douglas proposed a Medicare plan to give all residents of Saskatchewan free medical care. Douglas was a socialist, head of the CCF party. He was tiny, a boxer, a fighter, and my family knew him personally — his daughter Shirley went to high school in

[6]http://www.nytimes.com/2014/04/06/opinion/sunday/as-vermont-goes-so-goes-the-nation.html

Regina with my sister Estelle. In July of 1962, the Saskatchewan doctors all went on strike, to protest. It was a bitter strike. Imagine — no doctors, no medical care. The strike lasted three weeks. Douglas fought hard and even began importing doctors from Britain.

Tommy Douglas won. The strike ended around July 21, 1962, with the doctors' submission. And the idea spread from Saskatchewan across Canada, with the federal government mandating national health insurance — a program America needs but somehow cannot seem to attain. It is thanks to little Tommy Douglas that Canada has a workable, effective health insurance system that America needs so badly but can't seem to attain.

Jeff Bezos follows the money

Have you been following Jeff Bezos' remarkable reinvention of Amazon? Ignore his purchase of a new toy, *The Washington Post* — that isn't part of the reinvention.

Bezos is doing what many successful companies fail to do. As Peter Drucker explained decades ago, companies fail not because they do things wrong, but because they do the wrong things … they do the right things for too long until they *become* wrong. Amazon became a market leader in online book sales, then broadened to selling everything, was highly successful — and while it was successful, Bezos is reinventing it, a highly difficult task. ("If it ain't broke, why fix it? How many CEOs believe that, and their companies sink as a result.")

According to David Streitfeld,[7] Amazon Fire TV "is part of a multi-billion-dollar effort by Amazon to move from selling goods produced by others, (low margin), to presiding over the entire process of creation and consumption (downloads and streaming)."

---

[7]http://www.nytimes.com/technology/personaltech/tvs/overview.html

Amazon is now selling a device, Amazon Fire TV, that lets consumers watch Amazon's video library, as well as play games, on their TV sets.

Recall that very quietly, Bezos positioned Amazon as a major supplier of cloud services, leaving Microsoft, IBM and other huge technology companies behind.

Bezos is using what Bain & Co.'s Orit Gadiesh called "profit pools" — a tool that shows profit margins at each stage of the value chain, and asks senior managers to ask, 'where is the money [today]?' and 'where will the money be in 5 years? This is precisely what Bezos asked. His answer: creating download content. And he is able to move Amazon, with alacrity and skill, to where the money will be. Move to where the money will be is shorthand for "move to (innovate) where value creation is highest".

Bezos may well slip and fall in future. But until now, his strategic moves have been alacritous and visionary. And risky — he is not afraid to risk billions.

He's worth watching carefully, to learn how to innovate tomorrow even when what you innovated yesterday is a big success.

From idea to product: Crossing the chasm

When I teach entrepreneurship and innovation, I do a bit of theatre. I show my class a 'matryoshka' Russian nested doll set, and one by one assemble each doll, nested inside a larger one. I do this until I have 9 dolls on the table, down to the tiniest one. Then, I tell the story how one year, a sharp-eyed student asked, why nine? Instead of ten? And I discovered a tenth tiny-tiny doll, much smaller than a pinky fingernail. I had been unaware of its existence, inside the 9th doll, for years.

See this? I hold it up to the students. This is the idea. This is the fun part. This is the easy part. The hard part? Implementing the idea. Building a business around it — the other 9 dolls. Without that, that tiny 'idea doll' is of no value.

Prof. Daniel Nocera, Harvard University, is an example. He has developed an 'artificial leaf'. It's an invention that generates energy the way a tree or a plant does. "Light strikes a container of water, and out bubbles hydrogen, an energy source, as the light breaks H_2O into hydrogen and oxygen." How does this work? Writes Jack Hittmarch in *The New York Times*: "A silicon strip coated with catalysts breaks down the water molecule [using sunlight]."[8]

Wow! Hydrogen! You could use all that hydrogen to power fuel cells, which are devices that convert the chemical energy from a fuel into electricity through a chemical reaction with oxygen or another oxidizing agent. Hydrogen is the most common 'fuel' for fuel cells.

Big wow! But the discovery was made years ago. Nocera says his system is very safe. "My system is based on water, so if there was a catastrophe we'd just need a mop." However, hydrogen is highly flammable, and highly explosive.

So turning the 'artificial leaf' into usable energy means surmounting many obstacles. Create viable fuel cell technology. Solve safety issues, in storing hydrogen. Get consumers accustomed to using fuel cells.

There are many cheap reliable nonpolluting energy sources. The issue, it seems, is not the invention. It's how to make it desirable and usable for consumers. And THAT is a huge problem.

Nocera says that fracking and cheap natural gas is "killing" his 'artificial leaf' invention. But one day fracking may actually help. Fracking can produce hydrogen, but does so at a cost of producing carbon dioxide, which worsens global warming. If such hydrogen production becomes widespread, so will the infrastructure to use it. And then, Nocera's 'artificial leaf' will be popular, because it can produce hydrogen (to feed the infrastructure) without generating carbon dioxide. It will defeat fracking.

To sum up: There are loads of great new technologies that 'solve' our problems. But there is a lack of wise capable entrepreneurs who know how to commercialize them fast, cheap, good, friendly, easy... And governments willing to supply the needed infrastructure. Innovators should bone up on these technologies and invest creativity not in new ideas but in how to implement old ones and diffuse them widely.

Long ago, Geoffrey Moore taught us how important it is to 'cross the chasm' between early adopters of innovation and mass-market buyers. There is a different chasm, equally hard to cross — the chasm between a great idea based on sound technology, and a widespread commercial product or service used and loved by all. There is as much or more need

---

[8] www.nytimes.com/2014/03/30/.../the-artificial-leaf-is-here-again.html

for creativity in crossing this chasm as there is in inventing new technologies.

Entrepreneurial energy: It's everywhere — Sizwe (S. Africa) and Atef (Jordan/Syria)

My friend Prof. Dan Shechtman, Nobel Laureate for Chemistry (2011), has for over years been trekking tirelessly across the globe, using his Nobel pulpit to deliver a message: 'Entrepreneurship can change the world'. His infinite passion and energy, despite his age (72), reflects the infinite inexhaustible energy of entrepreneurs who seek to create value and build businesses. Here are two examples, both from the *BBC World Service*:

1. Sizwe Nzima: *"Collecting medicine from a hospital or dispensary in some of South Africa's townships can be a challenge — with the cost of transport and queuing times a problem for many people. Now one young man from Cape Town, Sizwe Nzima, has come up with a novel solution, which is not only helping patients in the community but has also seen him build a successful business."*

   Nzima identified a need: People in South African townships spent hours in queues, losing valuable work time, to get medicines from hospital dispensaries. Why not get the medicine for them, and deliver it, with squads of bike riders? How did he get the idea? He had to get medicine for his grandmother. Like many great startups, his began when he identified a very personal need, and realized others had the same unsatisfied need as well.

   Now, the 21-year-old has a successful business. Like all great ideas, you have to ask: Why didn't we think of that before?

2. Atef, wedding dress magnate: "The door of a metal cargo container creaks open to reveal a row of embroidered and bejeweled dresses in red, pink and white.

   I had stepped into Atef's wedding dress hire shop, a business that serves as a reminder that romance blossoms in the bleakest of environments. Atef's business in is the Zaatari refugee camp in Jordan, home to about 120,000 people who have fled the conflict in Syria. His container is located on a street that aid workers have nicknamed the Champs Elysees, due to the hundreds of shops and businesses. Atef has been in the camp for over a year now. He fled the fighting in Daraa, about 30 kilometers (18 miles) away in Syria. It is a city rich with businessmen thanks to a long history of cross-border trade with Jordan. "We started this as an abaya (robe for women) shop," says Atef. "Women used to come here and say they had weddings but they couldn't find dresses. So we bought two dresses for rent and it worked out well. "We have two weddings a day and there are people who come from outside the camp to rent dresses because it is cheaper here. "The profit is not that much but we are doing ok. We rent the dress for 10 dinars (around $14) whether it's people inside or outside the camp. "Sometimes we even take 5 dinars from people who can't afford to pay much."

Over a million refugees have fled Syria's brutal bloody civil war. They now know it will be a very long time before they can return home. Entrepreneurs like Atef are trying to make the best of it. His shop now serves not only the Zaatari camp but nearby residents as well. And he even has a Corporate Social Responsibility program, giving half-price discounts to those who lack the money.

The lesson here is so obvious. Governments everywhere: *Stand back, get out of the way, turn loose the entrepreneurial energy — and let Atef, Sizwe and other dynamic men and women create value, for others and for themselves.* If you can, governments, give them a bit of help, perhaps a few dollars. But at least, don't interfere with them. (The Arab Spring began, it will recall, when a corrupt bureaucrat tried to extort a bribe from Mohamed Bouazizi in Sidi Bouzid, Tunisia, on December 18, 2010, who scraped out a living with a vegetable cart.)

Entrepreneurship is like flowers in the arid desert — it sprouts and flourishes even in the toughest of conditions. Why not give it a chance?

Failure University: The diploma we all need

In my column for the fortnightly magazine *Jerusalem Report*, I wrote about Failure University — how almost all successful people have massive failures in their track record, and how failure is a stepping stone to success, as Michael Jordan always said. As the design firm IDEO says: "Fail early to succeed faster".

Here are two very different examples: Dov Moran and Abraham Lincoln.

Dov Moran is the Israeli inventor of the memory stick (also called thumb drive, or in Israel disk-on-key). His company M-Systems was sold to San Disk for $1.6 billion, an exit that made him wealthy. Retirement? No way. He then started Modu, which made the world's smallest (and perhaps first) smartphone, only 3 inches long. But Modu had a competitor called Apple (iPhone) …. And investors wouldn't back him. At 12 noon on a chilly November day in November 2010, Moran closed the doors of Modu. But he was unemployed for only 30 minutes. At 12:30, he was already in his new offices, a company called Comigo (TV/mobile interface), with some of his Modu veterans. Moran, now 58 years old, still works 20 hour days and flies economy to Japan, to show respect for investors' money and "to hang out with my workers". Modu's collapse led to at least 15 other startups, by Modu 'alums'.

And Abraham Lincoln? The man who led America out of the abyss of slavery, as the Spielberg movie shows brilliantly? Here is his record of failure.

- In 1831 his business venture failed.
- In 1832 he lost the election for the state legislature.
- In 1833 another business venture failed.
- In 1835 his future wife passed away destroying him.
- In 1843 his election to Congress was defeated.
- In 1848 Lincoln failed to win a seat in the Congress.
- In 1855 he lost the US senate elections.
- Trying for Vice President in 1856, he was defeated.
- Another attempt to run for the state senate in 1859 once again failed.
- Against all odds, he was elected the 16th President of the United States in 1860.

All those failures tempered Lincoln's stubborn steely resolve — he needed every bit of it to get the anti-slavery Amendment through Congress, after leading America in its bloody Civil War.

In Silicon Valley, it is well known — if you have 3 failures on your record, VC's regard you more favorably than if you have a clean record. The same is true in Israel. It does seem that what separates Michael Jordan, who said "I've failed over and over again — which is why I succeeded" from lesser athletes, and great entrepreneurs from mediocre ones, is not genius, but resilience and perseverance.

Harvard diploma? Great. Failure U. diploma? A lot better.

CHAPTER THREE

Break the Rules — Intelligently

Introduction

One of my favorite definitions of innovation is — breaking the rules, intelligently. The key operative word in that definition is 'intelligently'. Simply breaking the rules is chaos and anarchy. *Learning* the rules carefully, and cleverly finding which rules can be broken in order to create massive value for people, that is a different story. Like so many innovation processes, rule-breaking innovation involves an inherent contradiction. To break the rules intelligently, you must first learn them thoroughly. But in the process of learning the rules, it is very easy to become trapped — to invest so many cognitive resources, in learning the rules, that it becomes difficult to consider breaking them. Often so much intellectual capital has been invested in learning old rules, that it becomes difficult or impossible to discard them in favor of new innovative ones.

This is part of the psychological phenomenon of cognitive dissonance. In one experiment, subjects who were forced (or paid) to persuade others of a proposition they themselves disliked, ending up changing their beliefs in the proposition, to become much more favorable.[1] Learn the rules *too well* and it becomes much too hard to think about how to break them intelligently.

The pioneer of rule-breaking innovation is the management consultant Peter Drucker, who provided us with a template for methodically listing and organizing all the basic assumptions that underlie a business — and then, systematically, considering what would happen if the assumption were broken or simply ignored.[2]

One of the hardest aspects of rule-breaking innovation is that most 'rules' are not written or even stated. They are simply assumed. We all know that "this is the way it's done", because — it's always been done that way. That becomes an assumption that is hard to break because it is tacit, implicit, almost subterranean. The crucial part of rule-breaking is first to recognize the rules that are hidden or invisible. This exercise, when done in teams, is revealing and much harder than one might expect.

In a sense, this approach to innovation requires us to find a way to integrate the mastery principles of Confucius, the timeless Chinese philosopher and educator, with the rebellious principles of Steve Jobs ("think different"). Become an expert — and while you do so, challenge anything and everything you learn. Many of our educational institutions teach us to become experts. Perhaps too few challenge us to question what we are taught intensely, intensively, persistently. These stories, in this chapter, will hopefully help to remedy this.

Internet of Things: It's not hype

If you're like me, you may be skeptical of the term "Internet of Things" (IoT). I am tired of hearing about refrigerators that know how to order milk. This is not a compelling value proposition. But after reading a new

---

[1]L. Festinger and J.M. Carlsmith, *Cognitive consequences of forced compliance*, Journal of Abnormal and Social Psychology, 58, 1959, 203–210.

[2]Peter Drucker, *The theory of business*, Harvard Business Review, September–October 1994, pp. 95–104.

McKinsey Global Institute report, I am a lot less skeptical.[3] Here is a summary.

Definition: "The Internet of Things: sensors and actuators connected by networks to computing systems, to monitor and manage the health and actions of connected objects and machines, including people, animals and the natural world."

"The Internet of Things has the potential to dramatically improve health outcomes, particularly in the treatment of chronic diseases such as diabetes that now take an enormous human and economic toll …. Technology suppliers are ramping up IoT businesses and creating strategies to help customers design, implement, and operate complex systems — and working to fill the gap between the ability to collect data from the physical world and the capacity to capture and analyze it in a timely way."

"We estimate that the Internet of Things has a total potential economic impact of $3.9 trillion to $11.1 trillion per year in 2025. (At the top end, the value of IoT impact would be equivalent to 11 percent of the world economy, or $99.5 trillion in 2025.")

"By viewing IoT applications through the lens of "settings" we capture a broader set of effects…. a settings lens helps capture all sources of value — we identified nine settings where IoT creates value: Human (devices attached to or inside the body); Home (where people live); Retail environments; Offices; Factories; Worksites; Vehicles; Cities; Outside."

"Capturing [the potential of IoT] will require innovation in IoT technologies and business models, and investment in new capabilities and talent."

So: Innovator! Can you think of ways that connecting things digitally brings real value to people? Which of YOUR things would you like to see connected? Start with a setting; proceed to thinking of the sensors you need; and continue by thinking about how you would use the sensors' data to create value. This is a future industry waiting to be invented.

---

[3] McKinsey Global Institute. *The Internet of Things*: *Mapping the value beyond the hype*, 2015.

Why you are more than just one person

Meet "Clocky". You can easily buy one from Amazon. The idea is simple. Set the alarm for, say, 7:17 a.m. You are determined to rise early, jog, walk, walk the dog, write a chapter or do the dishes. At 7:17 faithful Clocky rings. But, you've changed your mind. You'd rather sleep another 30 minutes. Clocky, however, is clever. As you approach it, it runs away. Zoom …. You chase it around the bedroom …. Finally, you catch it, in a far corner … but — by now, you've awakened. No point in going back to bed. You're awake. Might as well get up.

Clocky is an example used by Prof. Dan Ariely, who hopefully soon will win a Nobel Prize in Economics, in a lecture given here at my university, Technion. Ariely has explored the nature of irrationality, and showed that we human beings are actually quite rational, or systematic, in our irrationality. For example, when we go to sleep, with good intentions to rise early, we are Person A. But when we awake, we are Person B, another person entirely. This is why we need Clocky. (Ariely notes that you can buy lots of Clockys on eBay, but for some weird reason, they have smashed tops and lack wheels.) And this is why we invent all kinds of ways to impose constraints on ourselves, because, when we choose to defer gratification, as Person A, Person B doesn't always manage to actually carry it out.

Person A and Person B date back to Ulysses, in Homer's epic poem, *The Odyssey*, who tied himself to the mast in order to resist the temptations of the Siren song. Ulysses "A" tied himself to the mast. Ulysses "B" sought to escape the ropes.

Just before Ariely's wonderful lecture (given by the way, without PowerPoint, simply with Dan standing in front of a packed auditorium, describing some of his wonderful experiments, interacting with the students, asking them questions, and in general, intriguing us with real-world economics about real people, facing dilemmas that we all face), I presented a research report on the pension crisis, with two colleagues. We recommended that each baby born receive a grant-at-birth, and that it be invested, for ... 70 years. With the power of compound interest, it will double five times, in 70 years, and the baby will be a millionaire ... and indeed, is already, at birth (albeit a future millionaire). That money cannot be touched for 70 years ... but when you know it is there, you have the secure knowledge that you will not live in poverty, when you grow old. This is an example of Person A and Person B, and ways to circumvent the conflict between Person A (spend, enjoy while you can) and Person B (save so life after retirement can be respectable).

What innovators learn from the Google Glass failure

Google Glass has failed. Google announced that it is 'going away'. From the buzz at New York Fashion Week, when fashion designer Diane von Furstenberg sported a red pair and sent her models down the runway with multi-colored ones in 2012, to the cancellation, many things happened. Much can be learned by innovators. Many lessons are found in *The New York Times* analysis by Nick Bilton, who broke the original story about Google Glass.[4]

1. It was not a failure. Perhaps there is no such thing as failure, in innovation. Why? Google learned a great deal. It learned, again, about the super-sensitive issue of privacy. Only a handful of people are concerned about it, but they are vocal and active, enough to sink a project. Some companies banned the wearing of Google Glasses in their premises, for privacy reasons. Who wants everything you do, see and say broadcast to the world?
2. Skunk Works: Lockheed ran a secretive Skunk Works operation in California, where its crazy inventors developed things that changed the world. Google had its own Skunk Works inside Google, Google X, even though you cannot imagine a more creative, open culture than Google's

---

[4]http://www.nytimes.com/2015/02/05/style/why-google-glass-broke.html?mtrref= www.google.co.il&gwh=A4990F3A1A4608082FB82E1F5420BF1B&gwt=pay&assetType= nyt_now

Mountain View, CA, campus. Somehow you have to protect the 'crazies' and give them space and freedom.

3. Interdisciplinary teams; Google Glass was developed by a weird team, with rock-star scientists and designers. Sergei Brin, Google co-founder, even joined the team. Having the company founder in the team helps a lot — gives it credibility.

4. Freedom: The Google X team did not have a predefined pre-ordained project. They themselves invented Google Glass.

5. Marketing: Google got to market quickly, but, through Glass Explorers, a select group of geeks and journalists who paid $1,500 for the privilege of being an early adopter. I think this was a good idea, in general. It applies Guy Kawasaki's principle, "ship, then test" ... get to market *fast*. But "the strategy backfired", according to Nick Bilton (who broke the first story about Google Glass). The product just wasn't even *close* to ready for 'prime time'. Reviewers described it as the "worst product of all time", noted its abysmal battery life.

6. What's love got to do with it? Yes — there was Cupid, involved, and he wasn't wearing Google Glasses. Sergei Brin became romantically involved with the Google Glass marketing manager, even though he was married, and the person he courted was one of his wife's friends. Vanity Fair reported the affair. Ouch.

7. Radical ideas are reborn, like the Phoenix. A former Apple product executive is working on a new and improved version of Google Glass. Someday, someone, maybe not even Google, will get it right. Apple's culture is far better at this than Google's.

Patents are like love: The more you give, the more you get

Some innovations change the way people think about doing business. Elon Musk, a great innovator (co-founder of Paypal, founder of Tesla, Space-X, etc.) has just announced that he is "opening the books" for all the patents related to Tesla and his electric car technology. Meaning? Anyone who wishes can use the technology he and his company created, free of charge. Just as Benjamin Franklin recommended.

What in the world? What happened to the assumption that if you create IP, intellectual property, then you have the right, nay the duty, to make huge profits from it?

And is this philanthropy? Or shrewd business strategy?

It is the latter. Musk wants to build Tesla. To do so, he wants the established big car companies, the ones who proved unable to develop truly great electric cars, to adopt his technology.

If they do, then Tesla becomes the first, the authentic, the real thing. And the way to make that happen is to offer the technology free of charge, and — reap the benefits indirectly. And I am convinced, the indirect benefits to Musk and Tesla will be enormous, far bigger than any royalties. Because an organization that sets the industry standards will ultimately dominate the market, patents or no patents.

We learn from Elon Musk that innovation is breaking the rules intelligently. Find a rule, e.g. patent everything that breathes, and see if you can break it, for your own advantage and the advantage of the world.

Are patents indeed like love — the more you give it away, the more you have?

Targeted drug delivery:
Promising new assault on cancer

One of my Technion colleagues, Prof. Avi Schroeder, Chemical Engineering faculty, has developed a promising new innovation for curing cancer. He heads the Laboratory for Targeted Drug Delivery and Personalized Medicine Technology.

"Being an engineer, I thought of an engineering approach to prescreen drugs on a personal basis BEFORE we begin a treatment cycle," he explains.

The idea is simple. It is like testing for an allergy, by scratching the skin and applying a tiny amount of the allergenic material. In Schroeder's approach, the cancer patient is given a battery of drugs, in miniscule doses — and then tested to see which if any actually reach the tumor, penetrate the cancer cells (which have clever defenses) and kill them. There are over 200 different anti-cancer drugs. Each individual may react differently to them, depending on their genetic makeup and the type of cancer they have, and even depending on their gender. (Thanks to studies done at University of California, Irvine, we now know that women react completely differently to drugs than men — and America's Food & Drug Administration now requires drug testing to include gender in the clinical trials, both for mice and for humans, to see if there are indeed differential gender effects.)

In his method, Schroeder creates nanoparticles containing drugs "barcoded" with DNA. The process of attaching DNA to each molecule of the drug is not expensive anymore, because DNA has become quite cheap. These nanoparticles are injected into the patient's bloodstream. They travel around the body and when they identify a tumor, the particles penetrate its cells through micro-fissures that cancer cells typically have. The drugs are then released into the cells. Some of the drugs will work and kill the tumor; some won't. To find out, the tumor is then biopsied, and cells are examined individually. The dead cells are separated from the living ones to see "which drug barcode is the most associated with killing cancer cells, and which are not."

So far, testing is in the preclinical stage. Schroeder is looking for financing to bring the idea to market. The beauty is, it is based on drugs that already exist. So time-to-market need not be as lengthy as for, e.g. new drugs.

How to build great ideas on key facts

How do you develop great ideas for startups (whether social or business-oriented), that truly meet unsatisfied wants and change the world?

I got an idea about ideas from a double issue of *TIME* magazine (September 8 and 15, 2014 double issue).[5] You get great ideas from one key fact. That fact at one fell swoop demonstrates vividly the need, and sets the stage for thinking big, for tackling huge problems with huge impact, if successful.

Examples?

- At present, 2.4 billion people are connected to the Internet; 44.8 percent of them are in Asia. That means that 4.6 billion people have NO Internet connection. How can this pressing need best be met? Challenge: Find a way to bring the Internet to 4.5 billion people who currently lack it.
- At present, 2.8 billion people in the world cook over open fires; 4.3 million people die each year due to indoor air pollution, caused by open fires used for cooking, which generate particulates that damage the lungs. Most of the deaths are women and children. Challenge? Find a way to save millions of lives, lost through inhalation of smoke from indoor cooking fires;
- Half the world's children go to schools without electricity. Challenge: Find a way to bring electricity to the 1.3 billion people in the world who have no access to it.
- Between 1998 and 2010, 463 children have died of overheating or hyperthermia in cars in the United States, the majority of whom were accidently left behind by caregivers. Challenge: Find a simple way to prevent this.
- 60 million plastic water bottles are used annually in the United States alone. Challenge: Find a biodegradable plastic, that degrades in 90 days, and that also fertilizes plants. (One of my students at Shantou University China, is close to a solution.)

* Apple has $158.8 billion in unspent cash reserves. Huge cash reserves are held (abroad) by Microsoft, Cisco, Google, Pfizer, and other U.S. companies. Challenge: Feasible legislation to get them to bring the money home and invest it in America.

And, one example of how this could work.

- Why don't we get heart cancer??? Because tumors grow when cells divide and multiply uncontrolled — but heart cells never split and multiply, beginning shortly after birth, unlike other cells.

---

[5] Available at https://backissues.time.com/storefront/cBackissuesTD2015-p1.html

Idea: Technion Prof. Yoram Palti thought that if you put an electromagnetic field around, say, the brain, when brain tumor cells tried to divide, creating a narrow cell wall, you could explode them with the magnetic field. This could treat 'untreatable' tumors and stop them in their tracks. Basis: Cell division is largely by sick 'cancer' cells. Palti, who is over 70, and his startup now have a proven device that stops brain tumors in their tracks, as well as lung cancer (very hard to treat). Check out "Novocure", now listed on NASDAQ. Thank you, Prof. Palti!

Why totally useless information is VERY useful

I'm reading Don Vorhees' 2012 book, *The Book of Totally Useless Information.*[6] In it, he explains the 'not-so-important' questions in life, offering over 200 explanations. Such as: why Scottish Highlanders wear kilts, why there are 7 days in a week, why the British drive on the left, why a left-handed pitcher is known as a 'southpaw', why pregnant women crave pickles, why keyboards are arranged as QWERTY, why are teddy bears so named, and was Dr. Seuss really a 'doctor'?

It's all really interesting. And it belies what the Roman philosopher Seneca said 2000 years ago: What is the point of having countless books whose titles the reader could never read in a lifetime? We do not have information overload, or useless information, or superfluous information — we *lack* useful relevant answers to key questions. We have too little *relevant* information, not too much. What we have too much of is noise — information that is not relevant to anything.

Innovative people, creative people, are infinitely curious. There is no such thing, for them, as useless information. Because, you never know what 'useless' piece of information will suddenly prove highly useful, in a

---

[6]http://www.goodreads.com/book/show/1371660.Book_of_Totally_Useless_Information

totally unexpected context. So, remain curious, and learn all the 'useless' things you can.

And, if you're curious — here are some of the answers: Scotsmen (never women) wear kilts, because they are practical, warm, and highly versatile. There are 7 days in a week, because that's what the Babylonians decided. The British drive on the left, because the buggy driver sat on the right and used his whip — driving on the right endangered pedestrians, who might be accidentally whipped. Pregnant women crave pickles because they contain salt, and because pregnant women need more salt, for their embryo (who swims in a salt bath). Dr. Seuss never was a doctor. And QWERTY? So arranged, so that typists had to type slowly, so that typewriter keys would not jam … And Teddy Bears? Perhaps I will leave that for readers to explore.

Any questions?

Innovation — "When", not just "What" — Daybreaker parties

Einstein taught us that the key to true creativity is how you frame questions, not how you come up with answers. James Thurber, an American author and humorist, liked to say that it is more important to know some of the questions than all of the answers. And someone else, I do not recall whom, said, it is better to have questions without answers, than answers that cannot be questioned.

The question we usually assume that launches innovation is: "What"? But rarely do we ask "When"??? In Israel, afternoon newspapers innovated simply by printing their newspapers and delivering them at 6 a.m. British Airways once tried serving meals on the ground, before the long flight, so people could simply go to sleep on the plane.

If you find a way to deliver a known liked product at a different and unusual time — this can be a powerful innovation.

Here is an example. Two young entrepreneurs, Matthew Brimer, 27 and Radha Agrawal, 30, are 'edu-preneurs'. They are engaged in educational technology. Their company General Assembly offers online classes, workshops, programs and education 'in the most relevant skills of the 21st C'. They had the idea of creating 'morning raves' — get-togethers held at 7 a.m., for two hours, before heading to work. Daybreaker parties have no drugs, liquor or other substances. What do you do? Mingle, chat, and dance. Why no alcohol? "The idea is not to flood the senses with external influences but to stimulate them through natural means. Through the music and body movement. All the senses are engaged." In other words — you don't need junk or booze to get high.

The parties are held monthly, midweek (usually Wednesday), each time at different locations, to those who signed up earlier by email. The idea is spreading from Silicon Valley (most of the participants are in high-tech, are young and without kids, so no need to make kids' sandwiches and get them on the school bus), and it started in New York City and is spreading to London, San Francisco and Tel Aviv (it debuts in Tel Aviv this summer).

Parties have existed for thousands of years. Change the time from midnight, to 7 a.m. — and you have an innovation.

What else can you innovate, by taking something loved, with a set time, and shift the time completely?

Innovation as grave robbing

One way to innovate is to rob graves; find old ideas that failed, dig them up, revive them, spruce them up and make them work. The British firm Hybrid Air Vehicles has done just that! The future may lie with airships like Airlander. This is a constructive form of grave robbery, in which crypts and tombs are raided for valuables, or even to steal the bodies themselves.

On Thursday May 6, 1937, the German passenger airship LZ 129 Hindenburg caught fire and was destroyed, when it tried to dock with a mooring mast at Lakehurst Naval Air Station, New Jersey. There were 97 people on board. Of them, 35 passengers and crew were killed, and a ground crewman. The tragic scene was broadcast live on radio, with play-by-play by a distraught broadcaster, who broke down and cried, on the air. The live account of the disaster spelled the end for hydrogen-filled airships. The trauma it created among millions made the word 'airship' anathema for decades.

Now, 77 years later, comes the revival. According to Matt McFarland, writing in *The Washington Post*, March 6, a British company bought a spy ship (helium blimp) built for the US Army, took it apart, shipped it to Britain, and is finding new uses for it. *The Washington Post* reports that "the Airlander is able to carry large payloads over long distances very efficiently. Hybrid Air Vehicles' project to develop the technology further is being funded by a government grant as well as private finance from individuals including Bruce Dickinson, the lead singer of the band Iron Maiden."

The company plans to build more of the airships; an Airlander costs about $40 million to build, and a version that could carry 55 tons would cost about $100 million. It is 300 feet in length, 60 feet longer than the biggest jets from Boeing and Airbus. It doesn't need a runway to land. It has four diesel engines and is helium-filled. (Filling the Hindenburg with hydrogen, highly flammable and explosive, was simply engineering madness. Helium doesn't burn.) The Airlander seats about 20 people and can carry between 3,300 pounds and 11 tons. And it uses 80 percent less fuel than a jet.

"There is now a worldwide competition to develop cargo airships," wrote Barry Prentice, a professor at the University of Manitoba in a recent paper. "The most important remaining barrier to a cargo airship industry is the lack of business confidence."

The long-lived ghost of the Hindenburg still lives. But, look to see many more cargo airships filling the skies in future.

The Einstein Principle in Innovation: Make time variable!

The painter Salvador Dali once painted a famous portrayal of time, in the form of 'rubber stopwatches'. It recalls Einstein's breakthrough in relativity theory — in his theory of space and time, time is no longer a constant, but in fact slows as the speed of light is approached. Indeed, a space traveler moving at the speed of light would return to earth to find everybody much older than he or she. In the century since Einstein proposed relativity, his theory has changed the world.

This principle has now been used to revive television. A few years ago, everybody was eulogizing TV (Rest In Peace), with low quality programming jamming the cable airwaves and viewer ratings plummeting. Amazingly, TV has revived. According to David Carr, Media columnist for *The New York Times*, there is a blizzard of great new TV and cable series. Here are a few: *Breaking Bad*, *Grey's Anatomy* (my own favorite), *Nashville*, *The Walking Dead*, *House of Cards*, *Modern Family*, *Archer*, *True Detective*, *Game of Thrones*, *The Americans*, *Girls*, *Justified* … and that's just a start.

What happened?!

Time changed. That is — that high-tech remote, with the red button now enables us to record and view later, or to access and view an entire season of 7 or 13 or 24 shows from a whole series at one swat. Time has become variable. That is, we no longer have to watch the program at the time slot allotted to it — often, in the past, the single most critical variable for a series success or failure. We can now watch a series whenever we wish.

There is a major lesson here. When you innovate, if you can shift the time at which a product is used, consumed or enjoyed, you can turn failure into success. So think carefully not only about your innovation but also about the forgotten question, 'when'? When is it used? When do people want to use it? When CAN they use it? Can I widen the range of (time) choice?

Television is the proof of concept. Welcome back, TV. As David Carr sums up, "the idiot box has gained heft and intellectual credibility to the point where you seem dumb if you are not watching it." Wow, what a change.

If you can subtract — you can innovate

Innovation is breaking the rules. But often, the rules most rewarding to break are unwritten ones, ones we assume are true in our heads, ones we never challenge.

One such rule: "Innovation is about *addition*" — adding new features onto old things. Nothing could be more wrong.

Innovation is about *subtraction*. Taking things away. Yet we use addition far more often than we use subtraction, in creative endeavors.

Here are some examples, drawn from Ruth Blatt's wonderful blog in *Forbes* magazine.[7]

* Led Zeppelin made an album, with no writing on the cover. Nothing, no band name, nothing. It was their best-selling album (Led Zeppelin IV). And they did it by subtracting.

* Composer John Cage wrote a piece called 4' 33", a four-minute 33-second piece in which a full orchestra sits down...and remains in perfect silence for over four minutes. A concert, minus the music. Insulting? Ridiculous? Usually, the orchestra gets strong applause when they stand up and take a bow.

* In 1966 the Beatles made a key decision. They decided to be a rock 'n roll band that does not perform for live audiences. By subtracting the 'live performance' from their art, they created new possibilities. They did not have to reproduce live what they did in the recording studio. They climbed new artistic heights in this way.[8]

Ruth Blatt advises, "Next time you feel blocked, try doing like the Beatles and take out something you used to think was essential." You'll be amazed at the results.

[7] http://www.forbes.com/sites/ruthblatt/2013/12/13/rage-against-the-regime-how-young-people-are-using-music-to-create-social-change-in-the-middle-east/

[8] But, did they? By continuing to perform live to this day, the Rolling Stones led by Mick Jagger have thrived and survived long after the Beatles came apart. The intimate contact with audiences through live performances seems an essential part of creating music. The rule is "subtract all but the most essential". But — what is 'essential'? That is often very hard to determine.

Creativity is breaking the rules — two examples

Creativity is widening the range of choices, often by breaking the rules — by doing things differently than everyone else. It takes courage and mental flexibility just to conceive of creative choices. Here are two case studies.

1. Disney Theatrical Group is initiating and investing in a Broadway musical production of the *Jungle Book*, first published by Rudyard Kipling as a series of stories in magazines in 1893–1994, and now a Disney property (like *Winnie the Pooh*).

    As director, Disney chose a MacArthur 'genius' grantee, Mary Zimmerman. Here is how she is building the musical. According to Rob Weinert-Kendt.[9]

    "… she starts rehearsals without a script, then works on writing one up until opening night …"! The new show opens July 1. It has already aroused controversy, because Zimmerman's setting is India, and she has been accused of (wait for it …) "cultural colonialism" (appropriating India's culture for capitalist profit)!

    Those who produce Broadway musicals invest millions of dollars in high-risk ventures. Disney has shareholders who track everything the company does. When millions are invested in a new show, without even having a script at the start of rehearsals … this is definitely breaking the rules.

2. Magazines have covers. *TIME* magazine has a different cover for each issue. New issue, new cover. That's the rule. It has been so for decades, making it even harder to change.

    Why?

    Why not multiple covers for the same issue? Why not, say, four different covers for the July 1 print issue of *TIME* — one new cover for each of four consecutive days?

---

[9]http://www.nytimes.com/2013/06/23/theater/the-jungle-book-comes-to-the-stage. html?mtrref=www.google.co.il&gwh=3F16035B12827BF0CF089D550571E303&gwt=pay

This is *TIME's* innovation, desperately struggling to gain new readers and keep old ones, in an era when young people get their news online.

Other magazines follow suit. *Fitness* magazine ran multiple covers for its July–August 2012 issue.

The point here is, ask yourself, what are the key assumptions? How does EVERYONE do something? Then ask, why is this so? How can we widen the range of choices, for ourselves and four our clients? Always, the point is not to do something new, but to do something better, to add value for clients. Novelty joined with its ally, usefulness. The difficulty is, people are used to old familiar things, and often resist anything new, anything changed. It takes courage to be an innovator, to widen the choices, to break the rules, and you have to be prepared to fail, sometimes massively. *TIME* knew this. So does Mary Zimmerman. We wish both great success.

CHAPTER FOUR

Innovation is a Team Sport

Introduction

Have an idea? Want to implement it? Probably, in most cases, you will need help. You cannot do it yourself. So, how do you choose a team? Build a team? Run a team? And what makes a team most effective, in innovation?

These stories provide some answers, and some ideas. There are a few accepted rules for creating effective teams. First, make them diverse. Find people with diverse backgrounds, expertise, disciplines. The wider the diversity, the greater the variety of perspectives each will provide. Sometimes, it is even recommended to add people to your team who have no knowledge or expertise whatsoever, in the particular problem being tackled. These people will ask 'dumb' or 'obvious' questions — and some-times, those are the questions that provide breakthrough insights. Second, keep your team focused. Team discussions should be open, free-wheeling — but at key strategic moments, responsible adults need to call time-out, and organize and refocus the work (this is a hallmark of teamwork at IDEO, a world-leading industrial design company based in Palo Alto,

California). Third, as the first story below notes, eschew hierarchy; drop job titles. It is unlikely that in a hierarchy, the top of the pyramid will have the best, most prolific ideas. Yet, that is often expected, dampening enthusiasm and motivation among those down at the bottom. There should be no 'stripes' or 'bars' of rank when ideas are being tossed into the air.

The last story cautions about a pitfall of teamwork: Groupthink. If you do assemble a team, encourage dissent. Consensus, widely praised, can often be a mortal enemy of innovation, as it directs energies toward the lowest common denominator, instead of the highest uncommon creativity.

Pile-on meetings: How to fight 'stovepipes'

Kathleen Finch is the chief programming officer of several cable TV channels: *HGTV (Home & Garden Channel)*, *Food Network* and *Travel Channel*. Her job requires a great deal of creativity, to keep programming fresh, relevant and lively for viewers.

Interviewed in *The International New York Times*, she reveals some of her methods for maintaining creativity. One of them is called "pile-on meetings".[1] I believe this is a remedy for stovepipe management — that is, narrowly defined management responsibilities, vertical ones, with very little interaction or overlap for creative ideas. Stovepipes are one of the reasons that big organizations with detailed vertical organizational charts struggle to innovate.

"I have a meeting every few months that I call a pile-on meeting," she told *The New York Times*. "I bring about 25 people into a room and go over all the different projects that are coming up in the next 6 months and the goal is that everybody piles on with their ideas to make those projects as

---

[1]http://www.nytimes.com/2015/09/06/business/kathleen-finch-get-better-ideas-with-a-pile-on-meeting.html

successful as they can be. The rule walking into the meeting is that you must forget your job title. I don't want the marketing person just talking about marketing. I want everyone talking about what they would do to make this better. It is amazing what comes out of those meetings!"

Another key insight? "I love when things don't go right, because it's a good time to talk about taking smart risks. If everything worked all the time, that would mean we're not trying anything crazy, and it's the crazy ideas that end up being the really successful ideas."

Again, another reason big organizations fail to innovate. Who would attempt anything, in the corporate world, that could well fail? Yet failure is nearly always a necessary stepping stone to ultimate success.

Creativity in the social network age

The Atlantic is a wonderful monthly magazine that has managed to survive when other magazines have disappeared. In a recent article "The Death of the Artist — and the Birth of the Creative Entrepreneur", author William Deresiewicz shows how much the process of creativity has changed in the modern age, focusing on (a) the influence of networks and social influence, (b) the need for diversity and versatility among artists, and (c) the need to 'market' your work and your ideas, as an active salesperson.[2] Here are some lengthy quotes from the article, worth reading and pondering. *Special thanks to a friend for alerting me to this piece!*

No more 'sole genius': "Creative entrepreneurship, to start with what is most apparent, is far more interactive, at least in terms of how we understand the word today, than the model of the artist-as-genius, turning his back on the world, and even than the model of the artist as professional, operating within a relatively small and stable set of relationships. The operative concept today is the network, along with the verb that goes with

---

[2] http://www.theatlantic.com/magazine/archive/2015/01/the-death-of-the-artist-and-the-birth-of-the-creative-entrepreneur/383497/

it, networking. A Generation X graphic-artist friend has told me that the young designers she meets are no longer interested in putting in their 10,000 hours. One reason may be that they recognize that 10,000 hours are less important now than 10,000 contacts."

Multiple artistic identities: "One of the most conspicuous things about today's young creators is their tendency to construct a multiplicity of artistic identities. You're a musician and a photographer and a poet; a storyteller and a dancer and a designer — a multiplatform artist, in the term one sometimes sees. Which means that you haven't got time for your 10,000 hours in any of your chosen media. But technique or expertise is not the point. The point is versatility. Like any good business, you try to diversify. The new paradigm is also likely to alter the shape of the ensuing career. Just as everyone, we're told, will have five or six jobs, in five or six fields, during the course of their working life, so will the career of the multiplatform, entrepreneurial artist be more vagrant and less cumulative than under the previous models. No climactic masterwork of deep maturity, no King Lear or Faust, but rather many shifting interests and directions as the winds of market forces blow you here or there."

The Democratization of Taste: "It's hard to believe that the new arrangement will not favor work that's safer: more familiar, formulaic, user-friendly, eager to please — more like entertainment, less like art. Artists will inevitably spend a lot more time looking over their shoulder, trying to figure out what the customer wants rather than what they themselves are seeking to say. The nature of aesthetic judgment will itself be reconfigured. "No more gatekeepers," goes the slogan of the Internet apostles. Everyone's opinion, as expressed in Amazon reviews and suchlike, carries equal weight — the democratization of taste."

It's About the Creator, not Just the Creation: "Among the most notable things about those Web sites (created by artists) … that creators now all feel compelled to have is that they tend to present not only the work, not only the creator (which is interesting enough as a cultural fact), but also the creator's life or lifestyle or process. The customer is being sold, or at least sold on or sold through, a vicarious experience of production."

Big disrupters

Disruptive technology is technology that completely changes the 'rules of the game' for established players in an industry — changes the nature of business, products, services, marketing or other key aspects of doing business and creating value. Harvard Business School Prof. Clayton Christensen drew our attention to disrupters many years ago. Established companies that ignore disrupters do so at their peril.

Here is *The Financial Times* list of the major disrupters of 2014. According to *Financial Times* reporters, "the range and number of individuals and companies that are upending business models around the world" is on the rise. … "the disrupters are everywhere".

1. Uber: Tim Bradshaw and Murad Ahmed have become "the poster child of Silicon Valley for disruption"; the five-year-old company revolutionized the taxi business in 230 cities and 51 countries without owning a single car, through its Smartphone application.
2. Alibaba: This online retailer, with $300 billion worth of online sales has transformed retail in China. It is now "snapping up low hanging fruit in overly state regulated markets" for everything.
3. Bob Diamond in Africa: He quit Barclays, and has now shown you can make money by investing in sub-Saharan Africa. He raised $352 million through an IPO in London in December 2013, and has done deals in Botswana, Mozambique and Tanzania.
4. Aldi and Lidl: They are disrupting the grocery market around the world, and Aldi is even exploring China. They have doubled their market share in the UK in the past four years. Aldi has opened 1,350 low-price stores in the U.S. and aims at 2,000 by 2018. Lidl too will soon invade the U.S. market.
5. Ford: Hard to think of Henry Ford's moribund car company as a disrupter, but the new F-150 pickup truck, with an aluminum body, never used before on a high-volume vehicle, is indeed a disrupter. To do this Ford had to replace arc-welders with new machines to screw, rivet, glue

and laser panels together. I remember another disrupter — Subaru, which made aluminum engines in 1973; I bought one, it was great, but was warned it would fail. Soon everyone was using aluminum for engines.

6. Tesla: last June founder Elon Munk offered to open up Tesla's patent book, which is very large, to rivals, "in the spirit of open source movement, for the advancement of electric vehicle technology". This was a clever move, not just PR. Munk wants the big car makers to adopt Tesla technology and boost the market for electric cars. Imagine if other large companies (Intel, IBM, Hitachi, Samsung, Apple) opened THEIR patent books so that everyone could use them free of charge.

Strategic coffee machines — creativity through chance conversations

The October 2014 of *Harvard Business Review* (October) has an interesting article by Ben Waber, Jennifer Magnolfi and Greg Lindsay, "Workspaces That Move People".[3] In it is an idea you can perhaps use. It's called Strategic Coffee Machines. Here is the story:

Jon Fredrik Baksaas, CEO of Telenor, a Norwegian telecom company, thinks that the strategic placement of coffee machines helped the company shift from a state-run monopoly to a competitive company with 150 million subscribers.

How?

Once, the company had roughly one coffee machine for every six employees. The same people used the same machines every day. Sales people talked to each other. Marketing talked to each other. The coffee was terrible — how can you afford good coffee when you need hundreds of machines?

The company ripped out the coffee stations and built a few big ones — one for every 120 employees. It also created a big cafeteria for all employees, rather than a series of smaller ones. In the quarter after the

---

[3]https://hbr.org/2014/10/workspaces-that-move-people

coffee-and-cafeteria switch, sales rose by 20 percent, or $200 million. Pretty good return on investment!

The basic principle here is simple: People in companies, or even in cities or in neighborhoods, just don't talk to one another. Especially people who don't normally need to, in the course of their work. Find ways to get them to rub elbows, and chat, and you can boost creativity.

I know of a case, told to me by MIT Professor Tom Allen, of a company with four labs, at the four corners of a floor. Each lab had a small office attached to it for doing paperwork. Simply by moving the offices to the diagonally opposite corners forced people in Lab A to chat with those in Labs B, C and D (they met at the intersections of the floor).

Once I visited a small Israeli startup called Hola. The founders observed that workers were crowding into a small kitchen to prepare their lunch salads. So they installed a dining room and full kitchen. Soon everyone was having lunch together (a healthy one) and incredibly important, useful information flowed within the company as a result. I've seen this in several startups.

Can you use the Telenor method? Can you use strategic coffee machines to boost creativity in your organization?

It takes two: creativity in pairs

Joshua Wolf Shenk has written a wonderful book titled *Powers of Two: Finding the Essence of Innovation in Creative Pairs*. An excerpt is available from *The Atlantic Monthly*, June 25, 2014 issue.[4] His point is simple: Very often, when two (different) people work together on an idea, the result is far better than when only one works on it.

Shenk goes into detail in discussing the collaboration of Lennon and McCartney These two Beatles created some 180 songs! Most of them are wonderful; most were recorded by the Beatles.

---

[4]http://www.theatlantic.com/magazine/archive/2014/07/the-power-of-two/372289/

Here is what Shenk observes about creative pairs:

For centuries, the myth of the lone genius has towered over us, its shadow obscuring the way creative work really gets done. The attempts to pick apart the Lennon–McCartney partnership reveal just how misleading that myth can be, because John and Paul were so obviously more creative as a pair than as individuals, even if at times they appeared to work in opposition to each other. The lone-genius myth prevents us from grappling with a series of paradoxes about creative pairs: that distance doesn't impede intimacy, and is often a crucial ingredient of it; that competition and collaboration are often entwined. Only when we explore this terrain can we grasp how such pairs as Steve Jobs and Steve Wozniak, William and Dorothy Wordsworth, and Martin Luther King Jr. and Ralph Abernathy all managed to do such creative work. The essence of their achievements, it turns out, was relational. If that seems far-fetched, it's because our cultural obsession with the individual has obscured the power of the creative pair.

My main 'take home' or 'take away' from this book? Find someone to work with. If possible, don't look for someone just like you. Find someone DIFFERENT from you, like Steve Jobs and Steve Wozniak, or Lennon and McCartney.

It takes two to (create the) tango

Not only does it take two to tango — it probably takes two to *invent* the tango. Tango probably comes from the Latin *tangere*, to touch, and it is a wonderful dance that was invented along the Rio del Plate, on the border between Uruguay and Argentina — and spread from there to the world.

Writing in *The Global New York Times* today (July 21), Joshua Wolf Shenk summarizes his forthcoming book *Powers of Two: Finding the Essence of Innovation in Creative Pairs*. His main point: The idea of a lone-wolf genius inventing breakthrough things is untrue. Usually great breakthroughs take two people.

He brings many examples: Freud and his colleague Dr. Wilhelm Fliess; Martin Luther King and Ralph Abernathy; Picasso and Georges Braque; Picasso and his fierce adversary Henri Matisse (sometimes, creativity emerges not from collaboration but from competition); Einstein and his friend Michele Besso, with whom he walked through the Swiss mountains and discussed his ideas. I would add Richard Rodgers and Lorenz Hart, a songwriting team.

"Two people are the root of social experience — and of creative work," Shenk argues. Why two? "We're likely set up to interact with a single person more openly and deeply than with any group."

I strongly believe this is true. When I embarked on writing a book on creativity (now available as *Cracking the Creativity Code*, SAGE India 2014), I felt it would be unbalanced, if I wrote it solo, as I had mainly an academic background. So I sought out my former student and current friend, Arie Ruttenberg, whose legendary creativity built a powerful ad agency. It was a wonderful collaboration, and our book was far better than if either of us had written it alone. We chose to preserve our individual 'voices' in the book, and hence identify the author of each chapter.

"The core experience of ... one entity helping to inspire another is almost always true," Shenk notes. I agree. So — if you seek ideas, if you have ideas, find a great partner. Preferably, someone very different from you. You'll see — it will greatly enrich your creative productivity.

The key to innovation in big companies: work together

Generally I write about books or articles that I've read. This time, I want to write about a book I intend to read soon, based on excerpts and interviews from Harvard Business School's *Working Knowledge* magazine. The book is:

Collective Genius: The Art and Practice of Leading Innovation, (Harvard Business School Press) was written by Prof. Linda Hill, the Wallace Brett Donham Professor of Business Administration, with Greg Brandeau, former CTO of The Walt Disney Studios and current COO/president of Media Maker; Emily Truelove, a PhD candidate at MIT's Sloan School of Management; and Kent Lineback, Hill's co-writer on her earlier book *Being the Boss: The 3 Imperatives for Becoming a Good Leader.*

Here is the main point: ".... innovation is a "team sport," not the act of a sole inventor. "Truly innovative groups are consistently able to elicit and then combine members' separate slices of genius into a single work of collective genius," the authors write. Or, as Hill puts it, "Conventional leadership won't get you to innovation." *The authors identified organizations with reputations for being highly innovative, then found 16 leaders within those organizations and studied how they worked.* ... the authors include narratives of executives within India-based IT company HCL Technologies, the German division of online auctioneer eBay, and the marketing division of automaker Volkswagen in Europe."

Here is the 'boldest' example of innovative leadership and teamwork, according to Hill. It comes from India.

- "Of the 16 leaders studied, Hill says Delhi-based HCL, under former CEO Vineer Nayar, might be the boldest. Nayar, who pulled the company out of a five-year slump, challenged the common belief that Indian companies provide low-cost products and services but don't innovate. "That (assumption) made him crazy," Hill says. "He said 'We can and will compete that way.' "Nayar focused on changing the organization from within, starting by empowering employees. In 2005, he told a team of 30-something young employees called the "Young Sparks" to develop the brand and a plan to change how employees experienced HCL. The group started with an icon, Thambi, which means "brother" in Tamil, symbolizing "the importance of the individual and the value of the collective" at HCL. Nayar recast his role as leader. He pushed for more transparency, adding 360-degree reviews for all employees and 360-degree feedback of his own work — he promised to resign if his own review dropped to a certain level. He set up a portal that asked employees to solve "my problems" and reported getting incredible answers from workers. From 2005 to 2013, when Nayar led HCL as president and then CEO, the company's sales, market cap, and profits increased six fold, according to the book. *Fortune* magazine wrote that the HCL had "the world's most modern management" and the company was named one of *Businessweek's* most influential companies. Nayar tells people, "I don't know the answers," which goes against the common belief in Indian business that the CEO should be a visionary. For Hill, Nayar shows the possibilities of what can be accomplished by an innovative leader who embraces a new style of leadership."

Big organizations ALL have trouble innovating. Perhaps Linda Hill's new book will help them figure out why and find a workable solution.

How to get a child to intensive care fast? Check out Formula 1 racing

If you wanted to benchmark world-class best-practice teamwork under time pressure — where would you look?

How about Formula 1 racing, where a pit stop to change tires can take only a few seconds (all four tires) or less? The world record time for the fastest Formula 1 pit stop to change four tires is in fact 1.9 seconds — hard to believe. For an amazing pit stop crew, that of the Red Bull racing team, see:

http://youtu.be/wZAw8cG9ZKs

In *The International New York Times* Julia Werdigier interviews Jan Filochowski, who heads one of the world's greatest children's hospitals, Great Ormond St. Hospital, London.[5]

He had a problem: How to transfer kids, after open-heart surgery, from the operating theatre to intensive care, super-fast (this transition is the riskiest part of the whole procedure). Here is how he defines the problem, and his innovative solution:

"In order to operate on the heart, we have to take the heart offline and operate on it for a while. It's incredibly risky, and the riskiest time is the transfer from the operating theater to intensive care. Everyone had done everything they could to get that riskiest moment down to 9.5 minutes, but they were thinking that this still was too risky. Then one of the staff said, "Let's look in a different area altogether. I love motor racing and Formula 1, where they manage to change all tires in a pit stop in 40 seconds." [Actually: a lot less!]... So we invited Ferrari and McLaren (two Formula 1 car racing teams), and they came and looked at our procedures. As a result, we reduced our change-around time by another 1.5 minutes to 8 minutes. It was very exciting. *It turned out that everybody needs a very precise task that*

---

[5]http://www.nytimes.com/2013/07/08/business/global/08iht-manager08.html

they do without any variation whatsoever. By applying those techniques, we were able to do something that was impossible."

This is creative thinking. Ask, how can we do this differently? Better? Faster? Who can help us? Look WAY beyond your nose, way beyond hospitals, to ... race tracks! Look for places where seconds are absolutely crucial (a Formula 1 race can be won by only a second or two).

No, you don't need to invent the wheel to be creative. Sometimes you just need to learn how experts change them.

Innovation is a team sport

Remember that old belief about innovation being, Inspiration! Eureka! I've got it!

Well, forget it. An article in *The International Herald Tribune,* citing serious research, debunks it. Those flashes of insight that seem like inspiration actually arise from complex interactions with other people. The implications for entrepreneurs are crucial. If you want to build a powerful innovation process, that generates more than a one-time idea (which in itself is never enough for sustained business success) — build a powerful team. Make teamwork a part of your company's innovation culture and DNA. And, by the way — forget about this brainstorming notion. Brainstorming — unfocused ideation — fails to generate usable business-grounded ideas.

Here is an excerpt from the article[6]:

- "Despite the enduring myth of the lone genius, innovation does not take place in isolation. Truly productive invention requires the meeting of minds from myriad perspectives, even if the innovators themselves don't always realize it. Keith Sawyer, a researcher at Washington

---

[6]http://www.nytimes.com/2012/01/19/opinion/the-key-to-creativity-solitude-or-teams. html?mtrref=www.google.co.il&gwh=3AC73F53F6CCDBDB04A3551CA16E72A4&gwt= pay&assetType=opinion

University in St. Louis, Missouri, calls this "group genius," and in his book of the same name he introduces a scientific method called interaction analysis to the study of creativity. Through studying verbal cues, body language and incremental adjustments during team innovation efforts, Sawyer shows that what we experience as a flash of insight has actually percolated in social interaction for quite some time.

- "Innovation today isn't a sudden break with the past, a brilliant insight that one lone outsider pushes through to save the company," he said. "Just the opposite: Innovation today is a continuous process of small and constant change, and it's built into the culture of successful companies."

- It's a perspective shared broadly in corporate America. Ed Catmull, president of Pixar Animation Studios and Disney Animation Studios, describes what he calls "collective creativity" in a cover article in the September issue of Harvard Business Review.

- "Creativity involves a large number of people from different disciplines working together to solve a great many problems," he writes. "Creativity must be present at every level of every artistic and technical part of the organization."

- So, we all should brainstorm our way through the day, right? Wrong. That tool, introduced by Alex Osborn in 1948, has been proved in a number of studies over the last 20 years to be far less effective than generally believed.

- "He had it right in terms of group process," said Drew Boyd, a businessman based in Cincinnati who blogs and speaks often about innovation. "But he had it wrong in terms of the method."

- Brainstorming, Boyd says, is the most overused and underperforming tool in business today. Traditionally, brainstorming revolves around the false premise that to get good ideas, a group must generate a large list from which to cherry-pick. But researchers have shown repeatedly that individuals working alone generate more ideas than groups acting in concert."

Instead of identifying a problem and then seeking solutions, Boyd suggests turning the process around: Break down successful products and processes into separate components, then study those parts to find other potential uses. This process of "systematic inventive thinking," which evolved from the work of the Russian engineer and scientist Genrich Altshuller, creates "pre-inventive" ideas that then can be expanded into innovations.

"The best innovations occur when you have networks of people with diverse backgrounds gathering around a problem," said Robert Fishkin, president and chief executive of Reframeit, a Web 2.0 company that creates virtual space in a Web browser where users can share comments and highlights on any site. "We need to get better at collaborating in non-competitive ways across company and organizational lines."

Teamwork? Or Groupthink?

In 1972 psychiatrist Irving Janis published a fine book, titled *Victims of Groupthink* (Boston, Houghton Mifflin Company). Janis used 'groupthink' to describe the dynamic that afflicted the Kennedy administration when the president and a close-knit band of advisers authorized the ill-fated Bay of Pigs invasion in Cuba in 1961. The President's view was that the Cuban people would greet the American-backed invaders as liberators who would replace Castro's dictatorship with democracy. His advisors 'heard' only reports that confirmed this view. The result was a disastrous wrong decision to invade Cuba. Many terrible strategic blunders have stemmed from such blindness and deafness, in the past, and doubtless will continue to occur, as groupthink drives decisions toward the lowest worst and most damaging common denominator.

• Formally, "groupthink" is defined as a type of thought exhibited by group members who *try to minimize conflict and reach consensus* without critically testing, analyzing, and evaluating ideas. Individual creativity, uniqueness, and independent thinking are lost in the pursuit of group cohesiveness, as are the advantages of reasonable balance in choice and thought that might normally be obtained by making decisions as a group. During groupthink, members of the group avoid promoting viewpoints outside the comfort zone of consensus thinking. Groupthink may cause groups to make hasty, irrational decisions, where individual doubts are set aside, for fear of upsetting the group's balance.

Avoiding groupthink is absolutely crucial when teams engage in innovation. There exists a difficult inherent paradox. Teams strive for intense smooth collaborative interaction. Often, friction, disagreement and conten- tiousness are frowned upon. Yet, when consensus is sought too quickly and too single-mindedly, the creative juices arising from fierce debate and conflict evaporate.

Ask yourself: In your teams, and in your organization, is there a strong groupthink mindset? What are the inherent dangers? Has groupthink led to bad decisions in the past?

How can you dispel groupthink by encouraging dissent, without ruin- ing teamwork and cohesion?

In this, as in other areas of innovation and creativity, there are no pat answers. Each manager must find his or her own solution.

One approach used successfully to avoid groupthink is scenario plan- ning. By encouraging team members to develop alternate, different sce- narios, the groupthink tendency to zero in on a single (usually wrong) forecast can be avoided, and the group can be motivated to consider other, seemingly unlikely scenarios.

CHAPTER FIVE

Innovate Everywhere, Everything, Everyone

Introduction

A modern fashionable adjective today, in psychology, medicine and social policy, is 'evidence-based'. This trend has so far escaped innovation. Much effort in innovation focuses on product innovation. Yet most new product launches fail, making the rate of return on such innovation rather low. In contrast, the rate of return on investment in process innovation is very high. This is because it is difficult to fail in process innovation — most processes can be improved, some marginally, some immensely, when effort is directed to do so. I believe China has created unprecedented double-digit growth for two decades, simply by discovering this secret and implementing it. But I believe process innovation is seriously underinvested by many organizations.

The key point in this chapter is that innovation is a mindset that can be profitably and effectively applied to every human endeavor, to everything we do and the way we do it. Organizations that quarantine their innovation to R&D departments are losing valuable opportunities. This chapter has stories about innovation in dark corners — in places where people and organizations usually don't think about creative ideas, such as how you price your product, the very first story.

The message here is: find a process, procedure, system, operations or function, that everybody does more or less the same. Think about how to do it utterly differently. Try it. If you fail, try the same thing again. The result can be world-changing — like the *Blackout* restaurant described below, where you cannot see what you are eating and dine in utter darkness — literally an innovation in a dark corner. The goal is not just to do things differently, but to do things differently in ways that *create immense value* for people. And often, the only way to tell if such value is created is to actually try it, try the dark corner innovation. There are a great many dark corners in our lives, where everything is done conventionally. By shining the light of innovation on them, sometimes the results can be startling.

The new pricing model: *Name Your Price. Really.*

Harvard Business School's *Working Knowledge* has an interesting piece by Michael Blanding, about research by Marketing Assistant Professor Shelle M. Santana. Santana studied "pay what you wish" (PWYP) pricing.[1]

PWYP? According to economists, it makes no sense. If you can pay, say, one cent, or nothing, why of course that's what everybody will do.

Yet another case where economic theory misleads.

"Research shows," notes Blanding, "that when people are able to set their own prices, almost everyone pays something — and sometimes well over the suggested price." Santana says she was interested in the broad variance of prices people pay, under PWYP, and who pays a little, and who pays a lot, and when.

She found that by controlling the environment and context, she can influence what buyers are willing to pay.

---

[1] http://hbswk.hbs.edu/item/name-your-price-really

Some examples of PWYP? Radiohead's *In Rainbows* album has 'name your price' downloads. Dallas Theater Center has *Pay What You Can* nights to attract new patrons. Boston Pedicab has an 'open fare' system. Panera Bread has four non-profit Panera locations with PWYP, noted in this book.

In one experiment Santana and a colleague designed a PWYP promotion for a pack of gum at a student café at NYU. At one scenario, their sign showed a pair of hands shaking, and read "It's Your Turn to Set the Price Today". At a second, the sign showed a group of hands in a circle that read: "Because We're Partners, It's Your Turn to Set the Price Today."

Guess which sign got the highest price? Of course — the second sign got an average price of 69 cents, compared with 57 cents for the first. That's a 21 percent difference. Why? It Creates a communal norm — pro-group, rather than just pro-self. Moreover, customers are willing to pay more, often much more, when a portion of the proceeds is donated to charity — something many companies discovered long ago.

Euro Disney pricing: Pure Mickey Mouse!

If you're a manager or entrepreneur, here is a 100 percent certain proven way to get into hot water. Take the advice of economists. I should know — I am one of them.

Euro Disney is a good example. According to basic microeconomic theory, if you segment markets and charge different prices, then you set prices inversely to the price sensitivity of demand. Low sensitivity? High price. High sensitivity? Low price.

Many Europeans buy Disney packages online. That means that Disney can charge people from different countries, different prices, because the Internet knows where you are. And of course, that's just what Disney does. Disneyland Paris practices "geo-blocking".[2] "For an identical stay, the Euro Disney website often offers higher prices on German computers than

---

[2]http://fromthegman.blogspot.co.il/2015/07/disneyland-paris-overcharging-foreign.html

on French ones." Euro Disney had 14 million visitors last year with pre-packaged prices. This year? Geo-blocking.

So what's wrong with price discrimination, if you're a monopoly and can get away with it? For one, it is not legal. The European Commission says national borders are supposed to be erased, and prices should be the same for all.

But worse than that — discriminatory pricing causes major resentment. Imagine that you bring your family from Berlin to Disneyland Paris, and find that your neighbor, on the merry-go-round, from Paris, paid half what you did. I know — it happens all the time on airplanes. Nearly everyone on the plane has paid a different price, from very high to very low.

Disney could say: If we charged one price, we'd have fewer customers, and would have to charge *everyone* much more to recover our costs. But this is pure Mickey Mouse!

When economic theory and profit maximization collide with basic fairness and empathy for customers, paying high prices, empathy should win. In the long run, it is simply good business. Beware of what economists advise. It is based on math, not on people.

Memo to all professors: Our monopoly has ended forever

Memo to myself, and all professors everywhere? Friends — you know that cozy monopoly that we enjoyed? Our courses, especially compulsory ones, were, like, the only game in town? We all paid lip service to teaching quality, but our promotions were based on published papers, most of them barely or never read by anyone? And I'm talking about myself here….

Those days are over. Here is how I know.

Thanks to an amazing support team at the Center for Improvement of Learning & Teaching, at my university, Technion, I offered a course on Creativity through the website Coursera: *Cracking the Creativity Code: Part One — Discovering Ideas*. Some 15,000 students from all over the world participated. It was a lot harder than I originally thought. I taped the videos three times, because the first two tries simply were not acceptable. As I write this students are now submitting their final project — a 2-minute video showing how they would use creativity to tackle seven challenges that we defined.

Unlike the wise adage "look before you leap", we leaped first and then looked. In preparing a talk for an academic conference on *Educational Technologies*, we summarized what we learned from our MOOC (massive open online course). We discovered that there are at least 50 other open online courses on creativity. Some are simply outstanding, given by the top people in this field, including Tina Seelig, at Stanford's new Design School. A Penn State course on *Creativity innovation and change* attracted 130,000 students.

It has now dawned on me, like a light bulb turned on, that the cozy little monopoly that I once had (and all other professors), is now over. Our students can now reach out and tap the teaching skills of the very best professors in the world. No longer do they need to suffer the inadequacies of the local substandard version. And if I, as a professor, do not improve very quickly, I will be as extinct as the brontosaurus.

Cracking the Creativity Code: Part Two — Delivering Ideas, is now in the works. And trust me — it is going to be a whole lot better. It has to be. Because my once-captive audience has been freed, just as Lincoln freed the slaves in 1864. My monopoly has ended.

And the world is a whole lot better for it!

Oscars: How to innovate (movies)

Many readers will have watched the *U.S. Academy Awards* (*Oscars*) on TV, when *Birdman* won 'best picture' and 'best director'. *Boyhood*, highly favored, lost out. But both *Birdman* and *Boyhood* featured extreme innovations, radical ones, ones built on breaking the rules.

Boyhood was filmed with the same actors during a 12-year period. It was conceived by the director Richard Linklater, and Patricia Arquette won best supporting actress. It is the story of a boy as he grows up to manhood. A 12-year production schedule with the same actors is unheard of in Hollywood …. Getting the actors to agree, and arranging the filming, was a huge and difficult achievement by Linklater. But it was crucial — switching actors would have entirely lost the effect. It just HAD to be the same people.

Birdman, with Michael Keaton playing the lead role of an actor who played a superhero (*Birdman*) and wants to stage a Carver short story on Broadway, was also a radical innovation. It was filmed in one single take, with the exception of a very few frames at the beginning and the end. This required meticulous production planning, long rehearsals, and a director Alejandro González Iñárritu who yelled 'cut' at any mishap during the filming, so that everything could be done in one continuous 'take'. Never been done, to my knowledge. The director is Mexican. Notice how many outstanding Mexican film directors there are?

Congratulations to *Boyhood* and *Birdman*, Linklater and González Iñárritu. I can only imagine how hard it was for you to 'sell' the two path breaking iconoclastic innovations, to producers and investors. Maybe you haven't made $300 million at the box office, like the film *American Sniper* — but you have shown the way for others, who will be similarly emboldened to innovate in future and make wonderful lively interesting and unusual films for us, that break the mold. Thanks!

McDonalds: The price of falling asleep

McDonalds, the $87 billion global fast food chain, is in trouble. The world has changed and its senior management team missed the bus. The price for this is heavy. The newly appointed CEO Steve Easterbrook, an accountant, will have to deal with slumping sales and a falling stock price. For years consumers have been opting for healthier food. McDonalds simply failed to meet or recognize the trend.

Here is how *Bloomberg Businessweek* describes McDonalds' decline under its previous CEO: "The rocky two-and-a-half-year tenure of Don

Thompson, Mr. Easterbrook's predecessor, was marked by flagging sales as the *company's key low-income customers continued to struggle in the wake of the financial crisis.* It also coincided with the rise of up market burger chains such as Five Guys and Smashburger, and the explosive growth of fast-casual restaurants such as Chipotle. …. Last year, McDonald's recorded its first annual decline in global same-store sales in a dozen years. The US, where McDonald's is the target of criticism for its contribution to the obesity epidemic and wage inequality, is not its only tough market. *Operations in Germany, Japan, Russia and China are also struggling.* Consumers are no longer interested in food that is simply fast — *they need to be convinced that it is, among other things, healthy, fresh and natural."*

McDonalds is an exceptionally arrogant organization, I am told. The global economic downturn began early in 2008; McDonalds could have seen that its customers would be pinched and less able to dine out. The trend toward healthy fresh fast food has been ongoing for years; Wendy's and Subway have leveraged it with great success. People simply get tired of the same Big Mac.

To me, McDonalds proves a core dilemma in management. McDonalds has great operational discipline in its franchises; it has to, to survive. But the same discipline destroys creativity, flexibility and innovation. Somehow, McDonalds has to revive its agility, its ideation, without ruining its fabled discipline and cost management.

Let's see if Steve Easterbrook, who played cricket in a British private school, will adopt a strategy that isn't precisely "cricket".

Business model innovation: Reinventing the supermarket

An Israeli entrepreneur named Iri Shahar has taught us a valuable lesson in creativity and innovation. Formerly CEO of a chain of retail stores, known as Fishman Group, he has just opened a new supermarket chain called in Hebrew, Ehad (One) with a simple basic premise: no-name (non-branded)

products, and only one non-brand for each product. One type of Cola (not Coke). One type of cottage cheese (NIS 4.90, about 20 percent less than branded cottage cheese). Many products in the Ehad stores are 10–20 percent cheaper than competing stores. At a time when Israelis are struggling with the high cost of living (higher in Israel by some 15 percent than in the OECD average, according to the OECD), Ehad serves an important social purpose. I am certain this is Shahar's goal — to make the cost of living lower for Israelis, while at the same implementing a new sustainable business model that generates enough profit to keep the business going and thriving.

Competitor Rami Levy, who some years ago opened a low-cost supermarket chain, pooh-poohs Ehad, saying that Israeli mothers will not give up their children's favorite brand name products. It will be interesting to see if he is right. I don't think so. I am frequently annoyed, doing the weekly family grocery shop, by the blizzard of types of cereal, shelves and shelves of it, most of it the same (Cheerios oat cereal are oat cereal, after all), at a variety of prices, some of them atrocious, confusing the buyer.

What do we learn from Shahar? First, as strategy guru Gary Hamel has argued persuasively and persistently, the most powerful innovation is not just in tweaking products or services, but in altering a business model or business design — how the product is sold, when, why, and to whom. Shahar's stores have only 1,000 products, compared with 15,000 for the average supermarket. Simplify! Second, it is a legitimate innovation to take an idea that succeeded elsewhere (Germany has Aldi and Lidl chains, that have spread worldwide) and apply it in your country. Indeed, this is great innovation, because a business concept proven elsewhere will likely succeed at home.

And by the way — Shahar pays good wages. He pays cashiers 25 percent more than minimum wage and stockers, 40 percent over minimum wage. "We want them to stay with us for a long time," he notes.

Why I live in *The House by the Side of the Road*

In Sam Foss's famous poem, he explains why he prefers *The House by the Side of the Road*, rather than the road itself:

Let me live in my house by the side of the road,
Where the race of men go by —
They are good, they are bad, they are weak, they are strong,
Wise, foolish — so am I.
Then why should I sit in the scorner's seat,
Or hurl the cynic's ban?
Let me live in my house by the side of the road
And be a friend to man.

As a management educator, I live (by definition) by the side of the road, rather than on the road, and I try to teach those with courage, creativity and guts how to navigate startups on the road of life and be a friend to mankind.

I've done this for well over 40 years. By Oscar Wilde's principle, "if you can, do; if you can't, teach"…. I teach and admire those who actually do.

Today, by the side of the road, two events made me exceedingly happy.

1. FDA approval was granted for the ReWalk device, by an Israeli, Dr. Amit Gofer and his Argo Technologies, an exoskeleton that enables paraplegics to walk and even climb steps. Dr. Gofer is a quadriplegic and cannot use his own device — but is working on a ReWalk version suitable for quadriplegics too.

An American veteran was interviewed on *National Public Radio* and he explained why it is so important for him to be able to stand upright — and how he dreams of himself owning a ReWalk device (it costs $70,000, at the moment — if America built one less useless aircraft carrier, every single one of thousands of U.S. paraplegic soldiers/veterans could have a device!)

2. In downtown Brookline, part of Boston, MA. I saw a *Big Belly* solar powered trash compactor. (See photo on p 90.) I teach this business case, about MBA student James Poss who won a business-plan contest and used the money in part to help launch this business. The Big Belly saves 3 out of 4 garbage truck trips, helps the environment, is very esthetic, and is simply cool. Poss thought he would sell them to ski resorts. None bought them — but the City of Boston did. Lesson: Get your product out into the market, as fast as you can, and people will tell you how they want to use it, and WHO wants to use it, and you will often be very very surprised. Until you get your product into the market, you will not have a clue about its true value-creating power. Remember: make your product an MVP — minimum viable product, and then launch it. If you wait for perfection, you will almost always be too late.

So — if I could, I would be on the startup road. But since I can't, perhaps a house close by the side of the road is OK, too. On days like today, it feels great.

Panera — innovation for people who have no money

Writing in *The Boston Globe*, Alyssa Edes tells us about Panera, a French bakery/café that has a new business innovation — give your stuff away, for free, or nearly free.[3]

For example, When Jonathan Diotalevi walked in to "Panera Cares", a new Panera branch near Boston's Government Center, "a smiling employee greeted Diotalevi at the door; he waited in line, ordered a tomato-mozzarella panini, and then asked the clerk, "So, can I, like, just give you two bucks?" Yes, he could. And he did, dropping the money into a nearby donation bin.

What? No prices? No 30 percent profit margin? How in the world can you run a business like this? *Fox Network* will scream that this is a Communist plot to undermine capitalism.

Here is how this branch works. "The restaurant at 3 Center Plaza may have been as busy at lunch time as any of the chain's other cafes nationwide — more than 1,600 of them — but there's a reason co chief executive Ron Shaich calls this one "a test of human nature." The non-profit

---

[3]https://www.bostonglobe.com/business/2013/01/24/panera-cares-pulls-high-donations/e9yyeEIg7VQi2Ip8MdN7aL/story.html

outpost of Panera Bread Co. doesn't have any cash registers, or set prices. Instead, it depends on donations from customers who pay *whatever they can afford*. The Government Center shop is the fifth of its kind for the St. Louis-based company — the first in this region."

Note: Some people pay *more* than the regular price. "I think it's awesome because it's obviously beneficial for people who are a little less fortunate," said customer Yanick Belzile of Lowell. "We can afford to, so we put in a little bit extra. If we can help someone else who can't pay for a meal, why not?"

"Wayne Gilchrist, who said he lives under a bridge in Cambridge, said he made a modest donation for a coffee and French bread with butter. "I'm homeless," Gilchrist said. "I got nothing and still gave because I want others to have."

About one out of every six Americans, or about 50 million, are "food insecure" or have trouble coming up with enough money to buy food, according to the US Department of Agriculture. "Many of those people work — some of them work two jobs," said Kate Antonacci, Boston Panera Cares project manager. "Hunger affects people of all types, so it's not only the destitute we serve."

When I'm next in America, I plan to eat at Panera. Let's support capitalists who get it, and who build businesses on the idea that people are basically trustworthy.

This idea could spread. What if businesses charged according to "pay what you can" and "pay what you think is fair", rather than "pay as much as we can gouge from you, to keep our rich shareholders happy"? Wall St. might never be the same.

Local empathy: Toilet innovation in Japan and Kenya — incremental excremental innovation

The core of innovation is meeting an unmet want or need in a creative manner. The tough part is simply identifying that need. Here are two examples of how empathy — feeling AS IF you were the person in need — is crucial. And how incremental innovation can be … excremental.

* A Japanese toy company, Toto, invented the otohime, or *Sound Princess*. It is installed in thousands of restrooms across Japan. What does the *Sound Princess* do? When you press the button (see photo), it mimics the sound of flushing water.

Why? Many Japanese women were continually flushing, so that the sound would mask the sounds they made in using the facility. The portable purse-friendly device is a huge best-seller in Japan.

I would *love* to know the back story, of how this device was invented and, more important, who invented it!

* The Umande Trust, a Kenyan community organization, tackled the problem of disposing of human waste in Africa. A common solution is the 'flying toilet' — plastic bags of human waste, flung as far as possible. Umande builds massive biodigesters that composts the output of a fleet of toilets. Each toilet charges a few pennies for each use, and makes about $400 per month. The biodigester composts the waste, creates biogas and makes hot water for some 400 residents.

There are probably millions of would-be entrepreneurs who are trying to devise apps, to rival *WhatsApp*, sold recently for $19 billion. The field is too crowded. I wish they would focus on dark corners, basic areas where there are unmet needs because, well, human waste is just not appealing. By empathizing with ordinary people, observing their daily lives, entrepreneurs can create value in areas far from the standard Smartphone. But, it starts with empathy, a keen eye and sharp ear, and a deep passion for making the lives of ordinary people better, even incrementally.

Twinkies are back!

Yes, it's official! *USA Today* (July 13), p 7A, informs us that as of July 15, 2013, Twinkies (cream-filled chocolate cupcakes) are back! And with a bang! There is a giant billboard of a Twinkie in Times Square. A new *Hostess* website with a countdown clock... A social media campaign in which people share their love of Twinkies. And a huge chocolate cupcake sign on the side of the Los Angeles Figueroa Hotel.

The *Hostess* Facebook page has 440,000 likes!

"It's the same Hostess, but with a different attitude," says Dave Lubeck, executive director for client services at Bernstein-Bein Advertising, which created the ad concept.

A truck tour is on the way. Promoters will travel the country passing out free Twinkies. It starts at Times Square on Monday. You will see Twinkie the Kid, the mascot, on the tour. Street teams are handing out "prepare your cake face" T shirts and "I saved the Twinkie" buttons.

Life can't be all bad, if Twinkies are back. Which would YOU choose? Austerity? Or Twinkies? Maybe we should send a few dozen to the sourpusses who run our governments.

Innovation can be simply bringing back something to life that is dead and gone, but was once beloved and has disappeared, and is missed. For many it is fresh and new, as they never experienced it. This is innovation at its best.

"Jugaad" in India or why to bet on India in the great innovation race

A friend directed me to an interesting blog by Neil Wilkof, IP partner at Herzog Fox Neeman, a leading legal firm. Wilkof's blog is titled: "Will "Jugaad" Lead the Way in Indian Technology and IP?"

What is "Jugaad"? Wilkof cites Wikipedia:

"Jugaad ... are locally made motor vehicles that are used mostly in small villages as a means of low cost transportation in India. Jugaad literally means an arrangement or a work around, which have to be used because of lack of resources. This is a Hindi term also widely used by people speaking other Indian languages and people of Indian origin around the world.

The same term is still used for a type of vehicle, found in rural India. This vehicle is made by carpenters, by fitting a diesel engine on a cart.... They are known for having poor brakes and cannot go beyond 60 kilometer/hour. They operate on diesel fuel and are just ordinary water pump sets converted into engine. The brakes of these vehicles very often fail and one of the passengers jumps down and applies a manual wooden block as a brake...

"Jugaad" is also colloquial Hindi word that can mean an innovative fix, often pejoratively used for solutions that bend rules or a resource that can be used as such or a person who can solve a vexatious issue. It is used as much for enterprising street mechanics as for political fixers. In essence, though, it is a tribute to native genius, and lateral thinking..."

Wilkof recounts his own "jugaad" experience in Bangalore, when his eyeglasses broke, and a cab driver stopped at a shop and fixed them with some adhesive.

Does "jugaad" remind you of creative improvisation, sometimes out of desperate necessity? This is thinking IN the box, literally.

The powerful vision of those who cannot see, the sharp ears of those who cannot hear: How Adina Tal changed the world

"...the human spirit has no limits —
except those we ourselves place upon it."

— *Carl Jung*

Part One: Eating in the Dark

Last night, to celebrate my 67th birthday, my wife, son and daughter-in-law took me out to dinner. It was, for me, an inspiring life-changing experience. I'd like to share it in this story, which will be longer than usual. If you have the patience to read to the end, all 3,500 words, I believe you will find it rewarding.

We ate at "Na La'ga-at" (Hebrew for "Please touch"), a center in Jaffa (south of Tel Aviv) that hosts thousands of visitors yearly to its theatre show, restaurant BlackOut, Café Kapish and special events.

Let me describe the meal first, at BlackOut, and then, the Center and its founder.

We remove watches with glowing dials, cell phones and anything else that glows. We enter a pitch-black room, guided by our waitress whom I will call "Dalya" — walking in file, one person's hands on the shoulders of the person ahead. Dalya seats us. The blackness is perfect. Earlier, in the light, we ordered. I choose "surprise" — dishes chosen by the chef.

Dalya has no problem serving us in the dark, because she is blind. She was born with failing vision, which later worsened. She can see light and dark, but no more. Dalya is indomitable. She works at BlackOut, and is a guide at the Holon Children's Museum, which has a "blackout" room to enable visitors to experience blindness. She travels, has friends, and uses her computer. She was widowed five years ago. Despite everything, her voice has a cheerful lilt, her face is luminous and she is boundlessly optimistic. And she knows my wife's blind student, at Haifa University, whom she identifies through the name of the student's guide dog. Dalya, too, had a guide dog, who died of cancer some years ago, a wrenching loss for her. Since then she has not had the heart to seek a new one, and moreover, since she travels, she would have to leave the dog with friends, perhaps burdensome for them.

Our son Yochai mentions to Dalya that he saw a film about a blind person who climbed Everest. Yes, Dalya says, he's here! He is a waiter here! And she invites him to our table. Ethiopian in origin, he talks about the extreme cold and altitude. He runs distances, with a friend, and he too has a happy lilt to his voice. Listening to him, I am thinking about what psychoanalyst Carl Jung once wrote, how the only thing limiting what we can do is the constraints we place on ourselves.

The meal is outstanding: asparagus in tomato sauce with smoked salmon, salmon-stuffed crepes, baked salmon with a spicy crumb topping, fresh-baked bread, Chardonnay wine, chocolate ice cream with cardamom seeds — all eaten in pitch black, using hands, fingers, fork. I find my eyes closing, as the dark acts like a warm blanket, wrapping us, enfolding us, relaxing the senses, focusing attention on the taste of the food (no visual cues to distract me), and the conversation too is wonderful, because again, our eyes are not constantly shifting and distracting as we talk and listen. I ask Dalya endless questions, fascinated by her spirit.

What one thing would make your life better? I ask. Accessibility, she says. Bus drivers should announce the number of the bus. Often, she recounts, I get on buses and find it's the wrong one, get off, and lose much time. [Her idea has since been implemented on buses quite widely.] Dalya gets around with a cane, and her memory is sharp — she remembers streets, curbs, and where things are in her home. And her hearing is intense. The brain compensates for one missing sense, vision, by sharpening the others.

As we leave, Dalya gives me her email address and we agree to correspond. Her face is radiant. I resolve to explore more deeply who innovated this remarkable Center and restaurant.

Part Two: Adina Tal Changes the World

Seven years ago, the curtain in the Na La-ga'at Center rises on *Light Is Heard in Zig Zag*, written and directed by Adina Tal. The actors? Twelve deaf-blind individuals, suffering from Usher's Syndrome, a progressive genetic disease, who until then lived in darkness and silence.

In 2004 the company tours North America, gains rave reviews in Toronto, Montreal, Boston and New York, and is sold out. Adina and the company do workshops for deaf-blind groups in Boston.

In 2005 rehearsals begin in a snowy village in Switzerland for a new production, *Not by Bread Alone*, with actors learning to knead Challah (twist loaf) for Shabbat. Actors learn to sense the vibrations of a drum, incorporated as cues in the show.

In September 2005 the group performs at New York City's Lincoln Center. A new dream emerges: Building a center of its own for the group, in Israel. A rundown hangar is located in Jaffa Port. Eran Gur and a dedicated team renovate the place, assisted by the National Insurance Institute and the Ministry of Welfare, along with private donors and foundations (including the Blechs). Deaf waiters are recruited for the Café Kapish coffee shop; blind waiters, for the BlackOut restaurant.

In 2008 Adina Tal is awarded the Chesed (Grace) Award at Israel's Knesset (Parliament).

Here is the story of how Adina innovated this remarkable play and center.[4]

---

[4]Taken from an interview by American playwright Michael Bettencourt, www.m-bettencourt.com

In late 2002, Adina Tal did not plan on founding a theatre company and a non-profit organization. She was already running a successful theatre company, busy writing, directing, and even acting, and felt that she had reached a point in life where "I understood what life was about." But underneath the satisfaction with her accomplishments buzzed a small desire to do something new, and when members of a non-profit organization that had just received a grant asked her if she would do theatre workshops with a group of deaf/blind people, to her surprise she found herself saying "yes."

When she walked into the room she noticed that none of the dozen people there noticed her because they had no way of knowing she had entered the room, "and this was my introduction into what being deaf/blind means." It also marked the beginning of a phenomenal story about theatre-making, human inventiveness, and the power of personal narrative. The surprise was genuine.

"No one in my family suffers from blindness or deafness," she said, and while she had seen her share of theatre done by disabled people, going to see it felt like "doing a good deed," and she never felt any need to go beyond that level. Yet there she was, driving from Jerusalem to Tel Aviv for her first meeting, partly hoping that something would happen to postpone or cancel this commitment about which she was having second thoughts.

Not that this beginning was easy or clear. A primary problem involved how to communicate with her participants. Each of them had an assigned interpreter/ social worker, and the interpreter would talk to his or her charge by signing into that person's hands. Shouting, gesturing, demonstrating, conversational interplay, the usual tools of a theatre director — Ms. Tal could not use them. So on that first day she formed them into a circle and simply began with physical movements — hand-waving, foot-stomping, and so on — to get them to feel their bodies in space and in relation to one another. On the drive back to Jerusalem, the initial sense of surprise had morphed into something else: she found that she had fallen in love with them.

After three months, events took a funny but decisive shift. Yuri Tevordovsky, from the Soviet Union, stated categorically that everything they were doing was "stupid."

"Why are we doing all this pantomime?" he complained.

Ms. Tal asked him what he wanted to do.

"Gorky," he replied immediately.

And how are we going to that? she persisted.

"That's your problem," Yuri shot back, "you're the director."

She answered that the problem was his, too, since he was blind and deaf.

"Okay," he agreed, in a tone of voice that said, "Well, let's do something together about this."

This "something" became Nalaga'at. During those three months, in talking with their interpreters before, during, and after their weekly meetings, Ms. Tal got the sense that while they genuinely cared about these people, these caregivers were often cautious — perhaps too cautious — in letting them engage with the world. When Yuri spoke out, and the others concurred that <u>they would like to do something more than what they were doing, Ms. Tal realized that they felt good in being pushed and not just accommodated. Just as any other artist would.</u> Including herself.

But as the idea of making theatre with them began to crystallize, she thought that while she wanted to do serious work, she didn't want to do Shakespeare or Brecht, or <u>have them resemble a deaf/blind version of a hearing/seeing company.</u> The source of their theatre would have to come from themselves, from their lives and their dreams.

And that was the spark that led to gathering material, writing, rehearsing, and eventually performing their signature piece known as "Light Is Heard In Zig Zag." Along the way, Ms. Tal and the others who worked with the troupe learned and unlearned a great deal about the (dis)abilities of their actors. For one, "I had always had this fantasy," she states, "that deaf/blind people were more sensitive to the world" and thus had greater insights and intuitions.

But she found that, at least with sufferers of Usher's Syndrome, who are not born deaf and/or blind but whose hearing and seeing decay over time, <u>they were not entirely used to their own afflictions and were often still learning after many years how to cope with the world.</u> In other words, they had their own "blind spots" just like the rest of us. But their sensory deficits did not make them feel like victims or pawns, or even necessarily handicapped.

One of the actors, Gadi Ouliel, has the desire to one day drive a bus. When <u>Ms. Tal learned this, she asked everyone else to board Gadi's bus in a way that showed something about themselves.</u> When Yuri Tevordovsky got on, he did so with a limp. When she asked him why he did that, he said he did it so that he could get the fare-reduction given out to disabled people. Obviously he didn't consider being deaf/blind a proper "disability"; it was so much a fact of his life that <u>he felt he had to add something on it to make himself appear more eligible for the rebate — something even a crafty sighted/hearing person might do</u>.

Another lesson, more pertinent to the making of theatre, came from Ms. Tal's realization that they lack an essential actorly skill: mimicry. In one exercise, she had each person take an actual grape and eat it. Then, using that sense memory, she wanted them to eat a pretend grape — and <u>she was astonished to see one dozen different ways of eating a grape.</u> Since none of them could see each other, they also could not copy each other — so each had to invent wholesale his or her singular grape-eating style. This excited the director in her because it made the act of acting fresh and innovative.

Unlike with seeing/hearing actors, who can rely upon past gesture-memories (and thus become lazy or derivative), Ms. Tal saw that they had to "re-invent the world all the time," and in re-inventing it, see it anew.

"There is an energy," she explains, "that I have never felt with any professional actor. I was discovering a whole new world." She also realized something new about noise, that is, the noise that usually accompanies any kind of theatrical process. "I'm sensitive to noise," she confesses, "and even though I myself always talk loudly, my concentration can get thrown off if there is too much of it in the room." In working with the company members, noise was obviously not a problem since communication had to be by touch. Thus, *everybody could become much more concentrated* on the work at hand, leading to a level of focus and deliberateness rarely achieved in more "normal" rehearsals. But perhaps the greatest challenge came with trying to find a way to establish with deaf/blind actors what is taken for granted in more usual theatrical circumstances: the umbilical relationship between actors and audience.

"Theatre," she explains, "is about creating a moment of meeting between actors and audience." But with deaf/blind people, "their sense of stage-presence is completely different." Until there is a touch of some kind — actor to actor or interpreter to actor — they exist in something of a limbo because they do not have access to any visual or auditory cues that place them in time and space. Only touch puts them in the present moment. *The challenge, then, was to create some form of virtual touch that linked the present momentness of the actors on stage with the being-in-the-present-moment of the audience.*

The problem solved itself in an unexpected and unforced way. For the actors, the more they worked and performed, the more able they were able to build a sense of audience responses (which Ms. Tal labels as nothing short of "magical"). After performances, they would tell her that they felt that the audience that night was "dry" or "non-responsive" or "warm." She didn't know how they knew this, but she knew their assessments usually hit the mark. In turn, the force of their confidence on stage spilled into the audience, which prompted the audience to react to the stage-action differently. Normally, the audience looking through the "fourth wall" of a play is an eavesdropper, a voyeur, at something of a distance. But watching and responding to a troupe of deaf/blind actors who cannot, in turn, respond to the audience's responding to them, forces the audience to rely less on the "outer" and to move more inside themselves, and this inward journey, in some "primary" way (to use Ms. Tal's word), blends with the actors' energies coming off the stage to create that umbilical so unique and essential to the act of theatre.

"I am not a mystical person," she avers, "but I also can't deny what I've seen — it is magical." (And another small but important discovery about applause. Ms. Tal realized that the actors would have no way to know when the *audience applauded them. So she devised a way of having the interpreters taps the actors' knees to indicate when the audience was clapping, and each actor would pass this tap down the line, hand to knee, hand to knee, until everyone got the message.) It took about a year to create the first performance of "Light Is Heard In Zig Zag," which puts the actors on stage with their interpreters as guides.*

Since then the production has changed a great deal without losing its core focus on the personal dreams of the actors. And these dreams, as Ms. Tal points out, are no different than the dreams "normal" people have about what they would like to accomplish in their lives.

- *There is Gadi Ouliel's desire to drive a bus.*
- *Yuri Tevordovsky "dreams that one morning he will wake up and take a look at the sky, and if the sky is blue, he will go fishing."*
- *Bat Sheva Ravenseri wants to become a famous actress and singer.*
- *Shoshana Segal would like someone to make her a birthday party.*
- *Zipora Malks wants to be a chief-of-staff in the army ("a particularly Israeli dream," Ms. Tal notes dryly).*
- *Marc Yarosky dreams of walking into a local pub, ordering a drink, "and being treated like a king."*

After each show, actors and audience have a chance to mingle and talk, and on a promotional DVD about the show, an audience member, during one of these post-show meetings, states that "I'm bewildered by the capabilities, how far humans can reach." And this sentiment of wonder and respect is echoed without exception by the audience members. As Ms. Tal says, "A lot of people are coming to see and hear us and want to be part of the group because they want to be near these people who had the courage to get up and do something." But current realities press in on these moments of revelation and acceptance.

"We are working on a new production," she points out, "that will use drumming extensively." Drums, she has found, have been an excellent way to build communication in the group because the actors respond well to the vibrations as cues for action. And this new production will risk more than "Light Is Heard In Zig Zag" because there will be no interpreters on the stage with the actors, as there are now. "Only drums," she says, "and cooking." During the performance, the actors will prepare and bake bread; the show's length will be the time it takes to complete that process. And, of course, at the end of the show, everyone will break bread with everyone else. (This new production has become 'Not by bread alone', and has been highly praised!)

Light is Heard in Zig Zag

A review by Michael Bettencourt of *Light is Heard in Zig Zag* , performed on September 15, 2005, at Lincoln Center's Frederick P. Rose Hall:

The stage in darkness. A double row of chairs. A voice — male, reverberant — speaks to the audience. Stage right a young man steps into the light, and his hands carve the air with signing. The stage brightens, and from stage left, in double single-file, the dozen actors enter, the one behind with a hand on the left shoulder of the one in front, guided in by the interpreters. They take their chairs. The performance begins.

It is a great performance, by turns mad-cap and touching, always committed and clean and direct. Each actor gets to tell his or her story — simple stories about simple wants and desires — and the staging of the stories, like the actors themselves, uses broad strokes to convey meaning: balloons, bubbles, blond wigs, blue cloth for the surface of a lake, over-sized foam-board cut-outs of flower bouquets, a pair of drums, and, at the end of the show, a sing-along. All of this is good the way good theatre is good: vaudevillian, unmawkish, inviting, unheady, clued-in — the jadedness cleansed away, critical distance cracked.

The most powerful pieces, to me at least, came when, at various times, one of the actors, stepping forward on the stage, the person signing to his or her left, the interpreter to the right at a microphone voicing a translation for us, "spoke" directly about being blind and deaf in a world not built for the sightless and soundless. We "able-bodied" in the audience, in an interstice between the rush-rush of our important day and how we have to get home after the show lets out to prepare for the next important day, are allowed to enter the space of "the other" and both forget about ourselves and remember ourselves, that is, drop the armor of ego and recover the power of a primary human-to-human connection by way of a shared frailty of being. We are all alike, like it or not, when it comes down to the struggle to make it all make sense.

This performance also has a second show just as spectacular as the first: when the actors and audience mingle afterwards. The lobby is jam-packed.

The interpreters, umbilicaled to their actors, sign furiously into the actors' hands as person after person comes up to offer praise and congratulations. Many in the crowd sign themselves, so while the usual post-show verbal buzz fills the air, pockets of gesturing humans create a kind of post-show physical buzz as well, the audience member singing to the interpreter who signs to the actor who signs back to the interpreter who passes it on to the audience member, all of this speeding along the way flocks of startled starlings wheel and spin through a cloudless sky.

We should support theatre like this — not because it's "feel-good" or because we want to soothe ourselves as "do-gooders," but because it is good theatre, that is, theatre that not only satisfies our aesthetic demands for craft and pleasure but also is enmeshed in, and drawing sustainable inspiration from, the world that faces it. Nalaga'at is embodied theatre, theatre from the body — not just from the bodies of the actors and their shepherding interpreters but from our bodies as well, a call to us to bind ourselves each to each, since *that is the only salvation we have as humans, and the only salvation worth having.*

Vive La Charrette! Get your innovation process "on the wagon"

Innovators can profit much from a clever process finding wide use in the United States and abroad in urban planning and development. The process is known as "charrette".

Here is how it works.

"Charrettes" often take place in multiple sessions in which the group divides into sub-groups. Each sub-group then presents its work to the full group as material for future dialogue. Such "charrettes" serve as a way of quickly generating a design solution while integrating the aptitudes and interests of a diverse group of people.

In urban planning, the "charrette" process is highly visual, with groups posting on walls drawings and pictures that reflect their thinking. The results are then integrated and combined. The process is not unlike that of IDEO's "Deep Dive".

For example:

...the University of Virginia's School of Architecture unofficially calls the last week before the end of classes "Charrette". At the final deadline time (assigned by the school), all students must put their "pencils down" and stop working. Students then present their work to fellow-students and faculty in a critiqued presentation.

The "charrette" is employed by municipalities around the world to develop long-term city plans, drawing on a communal process in which ordinary citizens express their views, often by bringing pictures or drawings of neighborhoods they regard as ideal. The "charrette" process is time-limited — the goal is to achieve consensus on a master plan within a very short period of time, and it is collaborative, avoiding the adversial legalistic approach that can take years.

The term "charrette" comes from the French for chariot. It is said that French architecture students studying at the famous Parisian Ecole des Beaux Artes scribbled desperately to finish their final designs while riding to school "en charrette" (in a cart). An alternate explanation is this: At the end of a class in the studio, a "charrette" (cart) would be wheeled among the student artists to pick up their work for review while they, each working furiously to apply the finishing touch, were said to be working *en charrette.*

The "charrette" method (www.charretteinstitute.org) stresses speed and urgency, overcoming often-fatal inertia and bureaucracy. It overcomes the political obstacle of individuals pressing their own ideas by making the ultimate solution a collaborative one, to which all have contributed.

Can you build a "charrette" process in your organization? Why not create an actual "charrette" (wagon, or 'chariot')? Roll it past groups, get them to place their visualizations on it, stick the results up on the wall — and then mobilize the group to integrate the ideas, back off them somewhat and create a final proposal that embodies the best features of all the various ideas. Encourage wild thinking, because ultimately, "feet-on-the-ground" wisdom will bring the ideas back to reality, in the process of integration.

Innovator: Don't just complain — do something! A man, a van, a plan.

A faithful reader drew my attention to a *Planet Money* blog about the key difference between those who complain bitterly and those who do something.

Adam Humphreys, who lives in NYC, wanted to travel to China. He filled out a long form, downloaded from a website, and showed up at the Chinese Consulate only to learn he had filled out the wrong form. At the nearby Internet café, where he went to get the right form, he found many others in the same predicament.

Reaction? #$%%%#%&*(!!!!!!!) Anger. Grumbling. And … resignation.

Not this time. Adam called his friend Steven Nelson. They rented a large Penske cargo van. They parked it in front of the Chinese consulate. And they mounted a sign: *Lucky Dragon Mobile Visa Consultants*.[5] Inside the van: Two Mac laptops and a printer, an old couch, "cozy as a dorm room". Confused visa applicants line up outside. Adam and Steve first charged $10. They were overrun. They then charged $40. Too high. So they settled on $20, with a $5 discount for Buddhist monks. Sweet spot! Just right. Just like *Goldilocks and the Three Bears'* porridge.

Adam says he can make $500 a day, but, he's cagey about disclosing real numbers. After all, someone else can park a van next to theirs. It's called capitalism.

How many times have I complained about bureaucracy, red tape, delays, incompetency, rudeness … and stopped there, rather than finding an initiative, taking action and offering a solution or work-around?

That, clearly, is the difference between an innovator and a complainer. Not IQ, brains, creativity, or anything else. Simply — willingness to act, to do something. Recall that da Vinci, that great creative brain, never actually built most of his amazing inventions, but simply drew them. Five centuries later, we venerate him, but most of us would like to change the world a little faster.

---

[5] http://www.npr.org/blogs/money/2012/01/04/144636898/a-man-a-van-a-surprising-business-plan

Restoring Lost Innovativeness

Introduction

In my nearly 50 years as an educator, I've taught many managers and students of management. With distressing frequency, I encounter young people who tell me that once, they were creative, but they no longer are, because they are paid well to do the same function in the same way, over and over and over, again and again, until the brains simply hibernate. In my courses, I challenge myself to destroy this idea, and to persuade my students that creativity becomes rusty but never disappears, and that the rust can be scraped off, like barnacles on the bottom of an old cargo ship, leaving the brain shiny, new and bursting with ideas.

To restore lost creativity, it is necessary to do regular exercises, just as we restore strength and endurance to unused muscles by programs of exercise. Indeed, to make my point, I often get down on the floor and do sets of push-ups, to show my students how the bicep and the brain are indeed similar.

This chapter contains stories about ways to restore creativity once thought to be lost forever. It isn't. One of the stories even suggests that our greatest innovation project is our own lives. As the world changes rapidly, we all need to reinvent ourselves, our skills and competencies several times during our lifetime. Each time we do this, our brains are stimulated to think differently.

If you feel bored, disinterested, stuck in a rut, consider making a change. Take on a new challenge. The result can bring an outburst of new thinking and a newly stimulated creative brain. You may fail. But it is not a true failure, because the effort itself will bring new skills, new knowledge and even new opportunities. Perhaps you can begin by using the "adjacent possible" methodology.

The "adjacent possible": Why one step sideways can become a giant leap forward

Steven Johnson's book *Where Good Ideas Come From: The Natural History of Innovation,* published in 2010, and his recent *Wall St. Journal* article, are both worth reading.[1] The title of the article summarizes its main point.

The secret to innovation is combining odds and ends. This approach was developed by scientist Stuart Kauffman, whose novel theory of evolution departs from Darwin and uses the brilliant notion of "the adjacent possible" — innovative possibilities that develop from existing products and ideas, that are close enough to be feasible and far enough to be considered creative. The 'adjacent possible' is a powerful notion, because it embodies the notion of options — innovative in ways that create the widest possible variety of options, or "adjacent possibles". Your innovation may fail, yet ultimately succeed if it opens a door to a powerful innovative adjacent possible.

Here are two examples, from Finland and India.

* Finland has a huge paper business, using pulp from its massive forests to make paper for Europe. But paper production generates environmentally unfriendly waste. So Finland found ways to mitigate the damage such waste does. Some of this research involved leveraging biotechnology. As a result

[1] Steven Johnson, *The Genius of the Tinkerer:* The *secret to innovation is combining odds and ends,* Wall Street Journal, 25 September 2010. http://www.wsj.com/articles/SB100014240527487 03989304575503730101860838

Finland now has a major biotechnology industry. Its "adjacent possible" was the industry adjacent to purifying wastewater effluents from paper mills.

* India's Kiran Mazumdar-Shaw's father was a brew master at India's United Breweries, who helped develop Kingfisher beer. Kiran wanted to study Zoology. Her father asked her to consider beer-making instead. Why in the world would I do that? She asked. Because, he said, it is a science. From a brewing enzyme business, Mazumdar-Shaw has built Biocon, a global biotech firm. According to *Bloomberg/Businessweek*[2]:

"Today the brewing enzyme business Mazumdar-Shaw started in her Bangalore garage in 1978 with 10,000 rupees ($1,200 then) has grown into Biocon, India's largest biotech company and Asia's biggest producer of insulin. Biocon is poised to ramp up competition in the $14 billion global insulin market, which is dominated by Novo Nordisk, Sanofi-Aventis, and Eli Lilly. Demand for insulin is expected to increase 20 percent a year through 2015 as the number of diabetics tops 285 million globally, according to market researcher RNCOS.

"In India's biggest drug supply deal so far, Biocon and Pfizer (PFE) in October agreed that the Bangalore-based company will produce insulin for the U.S. drug giant, which abandoned that business more than three years ago after taking a $2.8 billion charge on its Exubera inhalable insulin. Biocon will supply four generic insulin products to be sold initially in emerging markets, including India and Brazil."

"Today Biocon employs more than 5,300 people. Mazumdar-Shaw, 57, is India's fourth-richest woman, with a net worth of $900 million, according to Forbes magazine."

Lessons from Stephen Colbert — you can't discover the product until you're making it

Some readers may recognize Stephen Colbert as the host of the Comedy Central show *The Colbert Report*, which in its last season drew 1.7 million

---

[2] Adi Naravan, *From Brewing, an Indian Biotech Is Born*, Bloomberg/Businessweek, February 24, 2011, http://www.bloomberg.com/bw/magazine/content/11_10/b4218019885981.htm.

viewers, amusing them with Colbert's skill at deflating hypocrites and finding enormous irony in our daily political lives. CBS chose him to succeed David Letterman, in its *The Late Show*.

We can learn two major lessons from Colbert and his new venture.

* First, Colbert's persona for his *Colbert Report* show was entirely different from the one that he must embrace for *The Late Show*. For Comedy Central's savvy viewers, mostly young, "wonkish" according to *The New York Times*, he was perfect. Now, for *The Late Show*, he has to reinvent himself, to become more genial, softer, kinder, gentler, because who wants prickles at 11:35 p.m., when you're drowsy and just want to relax and doze off in front of the television? Jon Stewart, who until recently hosted *The Daily Show*, has said, "what made [Colbert's character] work was the thing that Stephen had to hide — which is his humanity". Adapting to your clients, when they change, is crucial for any innovator. And above all, it means being highly sensitive and attuned to who they are and what they really want.

So, that brings us to the second lesson, an important one.

* "You can't discover the product until you're making it". I would turn that saying into a sign and post it on the walls of every startup. Until you make the product, and deliver it to clients, and hear their reaction, you have not yet really discovered the product. Discovery begins not with the idea, but with the first person who actually uses the product.

So how did Colbert test his *Late Show* formula? He and his team spent the whole summer producing original content, and then uploaded it, even though they did not yet have a TV program to try it on. According to *The New York Times*, Colbert will have to "take command of his work and assert his tastes confidently and unapologetically" — this, at a time when there is an army of producers, directors, joke writers and CBS executives messing around with *The Late Show* (a machine that prints money) and giving advice.

So, innovator — discover your product — by making it. It's so simple. And it's why many startups fail, when they think they are taking time to perfect their product, without really knowing whether anybody will like it and buy it.

Be like Colbert. Get serious. Get your product out there and see the reaction. Before you do that, you won't have a clue. And above all — keep control of the creative process.

Freedom? Or security? Do we have to choose?

A *Pew Global Attitudes Project* asked this question, a few years ago[3]:

Which is more important?

Freedom to pursue life's goals without state interference, or state guarantees that nobody is in need.

The results: 58 percent of Americans chose freedom; only 35 percent chose security.

In Britain it was the opposite. Some 55 percent chose state guarantees and 38 percent chose freedom. In Germany, France and Spain, 62 percent chose state guarantees.

Here, in a nutshell, we have the reason why America has a great deal of entrepreneurial energy, and enormous social and economic inequality. And why Europe has a terrible dearth of entrepreneurial energy, and strong infrastructure and social safety nets.

In his *New York Times* column, Roger Cohen even goes so far as to blame America's obesity on the choice of 'freedom'. Taxing sugar-laden drinks would never fly in America. Raising gas taxes is a non-starter, even though the U.S. highways are crumbling.

Benjamin Franklin, that creative entrepreneurial American who invented public libraries and many other things, spoke up for freedom, in 1776. At the time, he was right. America's democracy had just been born. As a newborn baby, it needed strengthening.

But today? My question is — Are "freedom" and "social safety net" really, necessarily, perforce "either-or" choices? Must we choose? Are there examples of nations that have both?

Take Denmark, a very well off, prosperous European nation, wisely not part of the Euro bloc, which has very high taxation, superb social safety net and security, and a great deal of innovation and entrepreneurship. If entrepreneurs truly seek to create value, rather than become billionaires, they will not be deterred by high rates of taxation that generate revenues to support the safety net. If the wealthy earn 8 percent on their

---

[3]http://www.pewglobal.org/2007/10/04/chapter-6-views-on-democracy/

wealth after tax, park their money in tax havens, while the middle class barely earns 1 or 2 percent, is it not reasonable to allow the middle class access to the same privileges, the same 8 percent?

No, "freedom" and "social safety net" are not either/or. They are only if we believe they are. Freedom and social safety net can be both/and. That is how it should be. Now, the question, is, how do Europeans gain more entrepreneurial freedom without ruining their safety net, and how do Americans get a proper safety net without ruining their entrepreneurial energy? It's NOT that difficult!

Everyone deserves a second chance — let's try to help

Doug Deason is a wealthy businessman, president of Deason Capital Services and a philanthropist, head of the Deason Foundation. And he has a message.

When he was 17, in 1979, he broke in to his neighbors' home and threw a party, while they were out of town. (Actually, their son had given him a key.) The party got out of hand. The police were called. And Deason was charged with felony burglary. Note that word: Felony. A federal crime. You get a year or more in jail, in a federal pen.

If he were poor and black, his life would have basically ended. With a criminal record, he certainly could not have started a business in investments, or perhaps in anything. All he could have done was continue along the path of crime… after a youthful stupid mistake that really harmed nobody.

And this is precisely what happens to a great many young people in the U.S.

According to the U.S. Bureau of Justice Statistics (BJS), 2,266,800 adults were incarcerated in U.S. federal and state prisons, and county jails at year-end 2011 — about 0.94 percent of adults in the U.S. resident population. Additionally, 4,814,200 adults at year-end 2011 were on probation or on parole. *One percent of adult Americans are in jail. A large proportion are African-Americans. As many as 100 million people have some criminal record.*

Deason pleaded guilty to a misdemeanor (criminal trespass), paid a fine, served six months of probation — and then his conviction was expunged, and erased. He got a second chance. And he made the most of it.

Deason is a Republican. He and others are pushing for criminal justice reform. "Years ago, I made a mistake and got a second chance. Every American should be able to say the same thing," he says.

Deason's company has a policy of hiring non-violent criminals. He worked with the Texas State Legislature (not known as a bastion of liberal democracy) to pass a bipartisan "second chances" bill, that takes effect on September 1.

But I think there is another key point here. You really cannot legislate second chances. It is up to us, the people, to offer second chances, to forgive, and to help those who have made that one huge mistake and are paying for it forever. Of course there are risks. But when there is no second chance at a normal life, the only option is a life of violence and crime. Why in the world does America's criminal justice system not understand that?

How Vic Firth drummed up some business

Vic Firth died Sunday, June 26, 2015; he was 85 years old, lived a full life, and for an amazing 40 years was the principal timpanist of the Boston Symphony Orchestra. I'm certain I'd seen him in action, during the 20 years I taught as summer adjunct at MIT. He played for such great conductors as Bernstein, Koussevitsky, Leinsdorf and Ozawa. Seiji Ozawa called him "the single greatest percussionist anywhere in the world."

The Boston Globe once called him "debonair, affable, intelligent and sometimes cheerfully profane." And, by the way, he launched a company that bears his name that turns out 12 million drumsticks and mallets annually, used by classical, jazz and rock drummers everywhere.

How did this happen? Here is what *The International New York Times* wrote: "[he desired] sticks that were fleet, strong, perfectly straight, of even weight in the hands and able to produce the vast range of sounds he desired....Working in his garage, he whittled a prototype that had the lightness, versatility and equilibrium he desired, and engaged a wood turner to fabricate the sticks…. his students clamored for them [and] soon other drummers did too. Vic Firth Inc. was born."

A great many startups are born, when creative people want some product that does not exist, and take action to make it. They do no market research, no surveys…just introspection. Because, if like Vic Firth you want and need something and know exactly what you want, then other "percussionists" will want it too. And you don't necessarily need to be the world's greatest drummer to make it happen.

What would YOU like to have, that does not exist right now? Can you make one? If the answer is yes, then yes, you have a great head start. Go for it.

Innovators — are you comfortable with being uncomfortable? Are your kids?

Comfort: "a state of physical ease and freedom from pain or constraint".

The purpose of much of modern life seems to be to annihilate all sources of discomfort from our lives. Pain? Pop a pill. Hungry? Thirsty? You're never more than 5 minutes away from fast food that gives you bulges in ugly places. Frustrated? Well, if you can't leap over the bar, set it lower.

The problem with this is, things that truly create immense value for human beings happen, only when creative people become uncomfortable with the current state of affairs — with what exists. Without this divine dissatisfaction, and discomfort, we would have no progress at all. If everyone was satisfied with everything as it is…? If everyone shunned discomfort? Nothing would change. Nobody would try to close the gap between what is and what ought to be. And heaven knows, there is a lot that MUST change.

I think this issue begins with raising our kids. As parents, we want the best for them. We want them perhaps to avoid the hardships we ourselves experienced. We smooth their paths. We make them comfortable, as much as we can. And our schools do the same, avoiding the tension and frustration that occurs when kids are challenged to do better, far better, in math and reading.

It just doesn't work. The Jewish Talmud requires every parent to teach their children to swim. It's common sense — what if they fell into a river or lake? By the same logic we also must prepare our kids for life's challenges. Meeting those challenges may involve prolonged discomfort. If you cannot face any discomfort, how can you achieve greatness, for yourself and for others? How will you ever invest the 10,000 hours that Malcolm Gladwell says is the difference between mediocrity and greatness, in anything? If you only do things that you know will be comfortable, successful, you will miss many many wonderful opportunities for adventure and innovation.

I recall jogging with each of our children — three boys and a girl. They didn't always love it. But our boys have all done marathons (I've done two, NY and Boston), and all have taken on, and surmounted, major physical challenges that led to important achievements. I think that running with them when they were young may have helped.

So my message is: Get comfortable with being uncomfortable. Help your kids do the same. New and strange things by definition are uncomfortable, in general. If you welcome the risk, the uncertainty, the angst, that comes with trying the unfamiliar, the challenging, the unknown, even the frustrating, if you welcome discomfort, soon you become comfortable with it. And then, you can go on to invent great things and change the world.

Chaos is the new world order

Thomas Friedman's *New York Times* column helps us understand what is going on in the world. In a word: chaos. Chaos is the new world order.[4] Here is what he means.

---

[4]http://www.nytimes.com/2014/07/16/opinion/thomas-friedman-israeli-palestinian-conflict-order-disorder.html?mtrref=www.google.co.il&gwh=72A944B18187AE52717DC08 7513770E7&gwt=pay&assetType=opinion

Quoting a high-tech executive, Tom Goodwin, Friedman notes: Uber is the world's biggest taxi company but has no taxis. Facebook is the world's most popular media owner but has no content. Alibaba is the world's most valuable retailer but has no inventory. Airbnb is the world's biggest accommodation provider but has no real estate.

So what is going on? More and more businesses are simply doing global matchmaking (someone needs something, someone else has it), without owning assets. More and more businesses are digitally creating markets where none existed before. (You have a seat in your car? Why not use it to make some spare cash?)

This trend is highly disruptive, because it disorganizes and reinvents whole industries, in no time. The existing players (taxi drivers, hotels) have little time to adapt.

It's pretty clear, out of this chaos will emerge some order, and the chaos is actually creating value. But the implications are huge. A whole range of job skills will disappear. New patterns of markets and ownership will emerge.

For now, chaos is the new world order. How are YOU adjusting and adapting? Do you have a job skill that will be needed in a year or two, or do you need to reinvent yourself and your skills? If so, how will you do it?

These are interesting times indeed.

Feeling empathy for others: It's not enough!

In his *New York Times* op-ed piece, Nicholas Kristof mourns the death of his school chum Kevin Green. They grew up together in Yamhill, Oregon, and ran cross-country together. Kevin lost a good job, went on welfare, got divorced, became obese, lived on food stamps, got diabetes, and died at age 54. Tea Party Republicans say he "had it easy because he got government benefits without doing anything". Kristof notes that Kevin collected cans and bottles by the roadside, to make $20 a day for subsistence. Easy? Want to trade places? Did Republican wealth "trickle down" to Kevin and help him get a good job? Not a chance.

Kristof, in a later column, reports that he got immense flack from readers for this column. They said, it was Kevin's own fault. He brought it on himself. Those hard-hearted readers lacked empathy, he notes.

So do our leaders. It's no wonder. Did you know that half of all members of the U.S. Congress (House and Senate) are millionaires? How can they feel our pain, our middle-class pain?

We need leaders with empathy. Empathy — feeling the pain of others — is built-in to our physiology. We have 'mirror neurons' that enable us to feel what our counterpart is feeling at a given moment, not just pain, but joy, embarrassment, grief, happiness. But over time, we can easily turn off those empathy neurons, and rationalize them away.

But even strong feelings of empathy, I feel, are not enough. I found David Brooks' *NYT* column, written in September 2011, titled *The Limits of Empathy*[5]:

Empathy orients you toward moral action, but it doesn't seem to help much when that action comes at a personal cost. You may feel a pang for the homeless guy on the other side of the street, but the odds are that you are not going to cross the street to give him a dollar. There have been piles of studies investigating the link between empathy and moral action. Different scholars come to different conclusions, but, in a recent paper, Jesse Prinz, a philosopher at City University of New York, summarized the research this way: "These studies suggest that empathy is not a major player when it comes to moral motivation. Its contribution is negligible in children, modest in adults, and non-existent when costs are significant." Other scholars have called empathy a "fragile flower," easily crushed by self-concern.

In other words: It's not enough to feel empathy toward others. You have to ACT on your feelings and do something about it, even something small and symbolic, at least once in a while, so that your empathy muscles do not wither.

In our recent book *Cracking the Creativity Code*, we list 10 brain exercises to develop creativity. The first of the 10, and most important, is "Act, Don't Gripe". If you see something wrong, injustice, try to fix it, take action, at least once in a while. I know a friend, who always, as a matter of principle, gives small change to homeless and those who beg on the streets, even ones who are clearly running a scam.

I wish we had political leaders who were middle class working people. We really don't. Until we do, it's up to us. Sharpen your feelings toward others. Develop your empathy. But don't leave it at that. Try to act on it. If more people did that, maybe we wouldn't even need to bother with those millionaires in Congress.

[5]http://www.nytimes.com/2011/09/30/opinion/brooks-the-limits-of-empathy.html

Messy desk? A sign of creativity

Say, is your desk messy? Are you troubled by it? Try to clean it up regularly, and fail? Get hassled by your neat obsessive significant other?

New evidence suggests — hug your messy room, don't hassle it. It's a sign you have a creative mind.

Writing in the online magazine *NewsMic*, Tom McKay reports that "There's fairly robust psychological evidence that messiness isn't just symptomatic of poor standards or effort, but might actually provoke creativity".[6] He quotes psychologist Kathleen Vohs, who wrote in *The New York Times*, "being around messiness would lead people away from convention, in favor of new directions."

Here is the experiment she ran. To test this hypothesis, Vohs invited 188 adults to rooms that were either tidy or "messy, with papers and books strewn around haphazardly." Each adult was then presented with one of two menus from a deli that served fruit smoothies, with half of the subjects seeing a menu with one item billed as "classic" and another billed as "new." The results (published in *Psychological Science*), Vohs reports, were enlightening. As predicted, when the subjects were in the tidy room they chose the health boost more often — almost twice as often — when it had the "classic" label: that is, when it was associated with convention. Also as predicted, when the subjects were in the messy room, they chose the health boost more often — more than twice as often — when it was said to be "new": that is, when it was associated with novelty. *Thus, people greatly preferred convention in the tidy room and novelty in the messy room.* A second experiment with 48 adults found that subjects in a messy environment came up with ideas "28 percent more creative" while creating a list of unconventional uses for ping pong balls, even though the two groups came up with the same number of ideas. Vohs argues the results are clear: Messiness actually spurs creativity."

The point here is obvious. Creativity itself is MESSY, in caps. Creative people have messy minds that collect random pieces of information and

---

[6]http://mic.com/articles/103954/the-science-of-why-the-most-creative-people-have-the-messiest-desks#.y8d6YX544

find new ways to link them. Creative ideas emerge from disorder and entropy, not order. The ultimate state of order is the universe as it will be in a few hundred billion years: All the energy will have been burnt up, and the universe will be perfectly orderly, at a temperature of absolute zero.

So — messy desk? Enjoy it. Cherish it. And, nonetheless — do clean it up once in a while, if only for your significant other.

A new miracle drug called "give thanks"

This morning, I awoke at an early hour and as I often do, I listened to one of the least popular Israeli radio stations, despite (or because of) it being the most informative.

The person interviewed was a family doctor named Dvorah. She had practiced for many years, loved what she did, but was overweight and slightly discontent. On a trip to Barcelona, to the Picasso Museum, she saw a painting of a doctor and a patient, titled something like "Compassion". It led her to rethink her life, and reinvent it, because she felt there were pharmacies in medicine, and ten-minute consults, but no true compassion.

The result was a book, and a method, to help people become healthy and remain healthy, in what today is known as *Positive Psychology*. This new discipline is built in part on two very long medical terms. One is "neuroplasticity" — the incredible ability of the brain to change itself, for the good. The second is the daunting word, "psychoneuroendocrinology", which simply means that our thinking stimulates hormones that affect our bodies and our health.

Dvorah's message, simplified into 15 minutes for listeners, was this: Give thanks. Each day, give thanks for your blessings. Believe it or not, it is proven medically and clinically that doing so can lower blood pressure, stress and even LDL (bad cholesterol). And we have many blessings to give thanks for, especially the ones we take for granted (like, life itself, having all our limbs, our sight, hearing, etc.).

[Do you love, as I do, the Mercedes Sosa song, *Gracias a la Vida*? Thanks to Life. Now, we know that it is therapeutic!]

Dvorah recommends that families have dinner together each evening, and do a small ritual. Let each person thank someone else in the family for some small kindness done during the day. The result strengthens family bonds, and family bonds simply make us all healthier and happier.

It's that simple.

Here are the words (in English) to the last verses of *Gracias a la Vida*.... it sounds far better in Spanish...

*THANKS TO THE LIFE THAT HAS GIVEN ME SO MUCH
IT HAS GIVEN STRENGTH TO MY TIRED FEET
WITH THEM I WALKED CITIES AND PUDDLES
BEACHES AND DESSERTS, MOUNTAINS AND PLANES
AND YOUR HOUSE, YOUR STREET AND YOUR COURTYARD*

*THANKS TO THE LIFE THAT HAS GIVEN ME SO MUCH
I GAVE MY BEATING HEART
WHEN I LOOK AT THE FRUIT OF THE HUMAN BRAIN
WHEN I LOOK AT THE GOOD SO FAR FROM THE BAD
WHEN I LOOK INSIDE YOUR CLEAR EYES*

*THANKS TO THE LIFE THAT HAS GIVEN ME SO MUCH
IT GAVE THE LAUGHTER AND THE CRIYING
SO I CAN DISTINGUISH HAPPINESS FROM SADNESS
BOTH MATERIALS THAT FORM MY SONG
AND YOUR SONG THAT IS MINE TOO
AND THE SONG OF ALL WHICH IS MY OWN SONG
THANKS TO THE LIFE THAT HAS GIVEN ME SO MUCH*

Find meaning — even kids seek it

Writing in *The New York Times'* Sunday magazine Konika Banerjee (Yale grad student in psychology) and Paul Bloom (Yale psychology professor) make a powerful, simple point. *It is a basic fundamental human drive, to seek meaning — to find meaning in the events that happen to us, right from early childhood.*[7]

---

[7]http://www.nytimes.com/2014/10/19/opinion/sunday/does-everything-happen-for-a-reason.html?mtrref=www.google.co.il&gwh=DA331706BDF52DBAEE32C8CEEC870210&gwt=pay&assetType=opinion

In research to be published in the leading journal *Child Development*, the scholars found that: "even young children show a bias to believe that life events happen for a reason — to "send a sign" or "to teach a lesson." This belief exists regardless of how much exposure the children have had to religion at home, and even if they've had none at all." Other studies confirm that our search for meaning is independent of religious belief. Atheists, too, need to find meaning."

The researchers caution us that this desperate search for meaning — the belief that there is order and purpose in the world, that it is not 'aleatoric' (random) — can lead us into error:

"But it can lead us into error when we overextend it, causing us to infer psychological states even when none exist. This fosters the illusion that the world itself is full of purpose and design."

Sometimes, life is indeed random. Take the stock market, for instance. A lot of its movements are random. But 'experts' always find an explanation, mostly wrong.

In his book *Man's Search for Meaning*, Victor E. Frankl showed how finding meaning in the most desperate context (in his case, a concentration camp) can keep us alive. I often quote Apple guru and VC Guy Kawasaki, who counsels entrepreneurs to "Make meaning, not money". In other words: create value in the world, and the money will probably follow.

People who have serious illnesses, for instance, often seek (and find) meaning in their suffering. They emerge from the illness resilient, strong and hopeful. Meaning creates hope. And hope creates strength, often beyond what we could previously imagine.

So, continue to seek meaning. Find meaning in your life, in your relationships, in your startup. And frankly, it doesn't matter that much if you're right or wrong about your theory. And recall the two scholars' last line — finding meaning does not mean you become passive. The opposite — we MAKE meaning by our actions:

" … the events of human life unfold in a fair and just manner *only when individuals and society work hard to make this happen.*"

Does your doctor listen to you? But, *really* listen?

Does your doctor listen to what you say? I mean, *really* listen? And ask you a lot of questions?

I've just finished reading a fascinating book, *Reaching down the Rabbit Hole: A Renowned Neurologist Explains the Mystery and Drama of Brain Disease,* by Dr. Allan H. Ropper, and Brian David Burrell. (St. Martin's Press, 2014.)[8] Basically Burrell, a wonderful writer, was a fly on the wall, and wrote down stories about how Ropper figured out what went wrong with people's brains.

A key point Ropper stresses is this: The technology for scanning brains has advanced tremendously. MRI and CT scans reveal a great deal. But nonetheless, a great doctor still needs to listen to the patient, observe and ask questions. Dr. Ropper writes:

"Many [patients] have driven for an hour or two, even three, to [Boston], and they want to be heard. What they hope, what they expect, what they decree, is that we take the time to listen, because the act of listening is therapeutic in itself. When we do it right, we learn details that make us better doctors for the next patient. The residents may not get this yet. They are focused on diagnosis and treatment, on technology, on scales, titers, doses, ratios, elevation, and deficiencies. All well and good, I tell them, but don't forget to listen!"

Does your doctor listen to you? Really listen? If not — and who can blame them, many times they are required to see 6 patients per hour, leaving no more than 10 minutes per patient — try to find one who does.

As I've noted before, even in modern medicine, technology comes last, not first.

How competing for grants kills science — and scientists' motivation

This is the sad story about how a shortage of resources and the system of competitive funding of research grants through peer-review, is ruining

---

[8] The "rabbit hole" refers to the one Alice in Wonderland went down, into a magical and often surreal or unreal world.

U.S. science and killing scientists' motivation. I heard it today on America's *National Public Radio News*, in a report by Richard Harris.

Ian Glomski thought he was going to make a difference in the fight to protect people from deadly anthrax germs. He had done everything right — attended one top university, landed an assistant professorship at another. But Glomski ran head-on into an unpleasant reality: these days, the scramble for money to conduct research has become stultifying. So, he's giving up on science. Ian Glomski currently lives in Charlottesville, Va. He quit an academic career in microbiology to start a liquor distillery.

Why is he giving up????

Because to get grants, you need to 'tweak' safe existing ideas, so your peers will approve it; because if you have radical ideas, your peers who judge the grants competition will shoot them down, because if you succeed, those ideas will endanger the judges' own safe, conventional, non-risky research.

"You're focusing basically on one idea you already have and making it as presentable as possible," he says. "You're not spending time making new ideas. And it's making new ideas, for me personally, that I found rewarding. That's what my passion was about."

Glomski wanted to study anthrax 'in vitro', in live animals, using scanning techniques. Today it's done by analyzing tissues of dead animals. His idea might have failed. But if it succeeded, it could have utterly changed our understanding of anthrax and other such diseases.

In theory, peer-review of grants is fair. But it fosters extreme mediocrity. And as government funding of research declines, competition gets fierce (1 of 8 grant proposals is successful, and it takes long stretches of time to prepare one — so young scientists spend their time writing proposals rather than doing effective research).

Harris reports that "…. payoffs in science come from out of the blue — oddball ideas or unexpected byways. Glomski says that's what research was like for him as he was getting his Ph.D. at the University of California, Berkeley. His lab leader there got funding to probe the frontiers. But Glomski sees that farsighted approach disappearing today." Playing it safe will never generate the creative breakthroughs we need.

As with many things in America, the competition for funds in scientific research is utterly messed up. And it is unlike to change in the near future.

How must entrepreneurs treat failure?
A practical solution

Recently, I spoke to a group of Brazilian entrepreneurs, while in Sao Paulo, at an accelerator, Startup Farm, run very well by Alan Leite. In the latest round, over 130 projects have been through Alan's capable hands.

In my brief talk, I tried to practice what I preach, and listened carefully to precisely which messages I brought resonated. The key one, by far? About failure. Entrepreneurship is less about success than about failure, how you perceive it, how you treat it, and how society relates to it. There are cultures where failure is treated as a personal crime; those cultures will never ever have entrepreneurs.

My wife Sharona, a psychologist, listened to my talk and gave me valuable feedback afterward. She reminded me of work by Stanford Psychology Professor Carol Dweck, who has done pioneering work on 'mindset'.

Here is a brief summary, in the context of startup failure.

Mindset is a mental attitude that determines how you respond to situations. There are two types of mindsets. One is a fixed mindset, which assumes that intelligence is a fixed trait, and that all our qualities and capabilities are fixed, constant and constrained. The second is a growth mindset, which assumes that intelligence (and other capabilities) are qualities that change, grow and develop, especially when we work hard at it. Why don't we see unmotivated babies? Dweck asks. Because when babies learn to walk, stumbling is not failure, it is a vital step on the road to success…and because you have to learn to walk, you have to stumble and fall until you do. Absolutely true of entrepreneurs, too.

Entrepreneurs should have a growth mindset. And they should use it to shape their perception of failure.

Failure can be regarded as *personal*: I personally have failed. Or worse, I myself AM a failure. My startup failed; I am a failure.

Wrong. Wrong. Wrong.

Failure can be regarded as a learning experience; my startup failed, but I am a brave and courageous entrepreneur, because I attempted something very challenging, and did not succeed, but learned a great deal, and eventually I WILL succeed to change the world.

This is how entrepreneurs, and all of society around them, should, can and MUST interpret failure. It is part of a growth mindset; failure is a step toward success. Thomas Edison actually said that, when he tried 10,000 experiments to invent the filament of a light bulb, and each failure brought him closer to the final successful answer.

Here is how Carol Dweck advises us to develop a growth mindset: *1. Learn learn learn 2. Realize hard work is key 3. Face setbacks. Focus on effort, struggle, persistence despite setbacks. Choose difficult tasks. Focus on strategies. Reflect on different strategies that work or don't work. Focus on learning and improving. Seek challenges. Work hard.*

Thank you Professor Dweck!

Technology comes last!

When my wife and I were in Brazil, I gave a seminar at the University of Sao Paulo, titled "Technology Comes Last, Not First". This was *chutzpah*, impudence, because it was a seminar for Management of Technology. When you see a surgeon with a medical problem, they often recommend surgery. Naturally. When you study Management of Technology, they teach you — well, how to manage technology.

But the audience got the message and understood. And it is so simple.

Great startups begin by identifying an unmet need. This is done not by asking people what they need, but by keen close detailed zoom-in observation and listening — not a skill engineers tend to have. Only after a clear unmet need is identified, should technology be pulled in, and only technology that can simply, quickly and appropriately be applied to meet the need, as part of a sustainable business.

I've seen countless startups driven by genius engineers, who create magical technology (recall Arthur Clarke, "truly advanced technology is indistinguishable from magic"), and launch a startup, and — their technology meets needs that do not exist at all.

How do you find a true need? Maybe, you yourself need it. And if so, others do too. Spanx started when Susan Blakely needed something to tuck in her bottom. The technology? Spandex. She made a batch and knocked on doors until it began to sell. She's now a billionaire. Lady Gaga records new songs after exhausting performances, in her bus. Technology? Her engineers insist, you cannot record high-quality sound in a bus. Lady Gaga? DO IT!! Because she needs the inspiration and immediacy of her audience. Sound studios are sterile.

The paradox is: Technology-driven startups cannot be led by, driven by, and directed by, technology, even though they are generally led by engineers. The principle is: Start with Why? Why make this? Who needs it? Why do they need it? Only if you have very strong clear answers, can you proceed to the technology that will satisfy it. This is so simple. Yet violated by many businesses and entrepreneurs, for big and small companies.

Think BIG

Yesterday I spoke to a group of entrepreneurs, at the University of Sao Paulo, hosted by Prof. Fabio Kon. The gathering was initiated by students, and it was organized in an interesting manner. Each participant identified himself or herself in one of three categories, using colored badges: criacao (creative ideas); negocios (manager or business person); and desenvolvedor (developer, or entrepreneur). There were very few "criacaos", but lots of negocios and desenvolvedor.

My main message to them was "think big". If you're going to invest years of your life in working on implementing an idea, it should be a big one, not an 8 percent improvement in something that already exists.

There are three avenues for 'thinking big'. I illustrate it using diagrams:

X axis: number of people you affect. Y axis: amount of value you create for each, on average.

One: Make a huge improvement in life; create huge value, for a huge number of people. Example: Jack Noyes inventing the integrated circuit. Or a cure/preventative for malaria.

```
#########################
#########################
#########################
#########################
```

Two: Make a huge improvement in life; create huge value, for a relatively small number of people. Example: Vaccine for a rare disease.

```
$$$$
$$$$
$$$$
$$$$
$$$$
$$$$
$$$$
```

Three: Create fairly small value for a very large number of people. Example: iPhone.

```
****************************************************
****************************************************
```

In other words: a huge fat rectangle; a thin tall rectangle; or a short wide rectangle.

But somehow — something needs to be big, either the value you create or the number of people you affect, or both. Why?

Because big ideas attract people with big abilities. Because big ideas generate energy and passion you need to implement them. Because we need big ideas to fix big problems, when small ideas will just not do the job.

Persuaded? Do you have a big idea?

The three intersecting circles of innovation

My attention was recently drawn to a three-year-old report, done by MIT scholars, for the health science research community. The report is *The*

Third Revolution: The Convergence of the Life Sciences, Physical Sciences and Engineering.[9] The authors, who include stellar figures like Profs. Phillip Sharp and Robert Langer, argue that "convergence will be the emerging paradigm for how medical research will be conducted in the future."

In order for this convergence to happen, they say, we will need "not simply collaboration between disciplines but true disciplinary integration."

Today, the structure of nearly all the universities in the world is obsolete, ancient, creaky and counterproductive. It is based on faculties, which are silos that work in direct opposition to convergence. The exceptions are research institutes that are cross-disciplinary, specifically nanotechnology. My university has a Nanotechnology Center that draws scholars from many disciplines, and the resulting integration has been tremendously productive. A small example: Prof. Hossam Haick, whose discipline is chemical engineering, but who has harnessed nanotechnology, electronics, chemistry, physics and engineering to produce an 'electronic nose', which can sniff cancer molecules, for instance.

Structure is not strategy, it is sometimes said. But, sometimes it is. Let's change the structure of universities. Let's find a way to restructure them, so that each faculty member has a very clear area of expertise, a clearly-defined discipline, but also has broad knowledge of other fields and above all, works as part of a convergence interdisciplinary team. And for this to work, their offices have to be adjacent.... Despite IT and networking, nothing beats face-to-face conversations over coffee.

Convergence poses a big challenge to those who would innovate. You need to achieve two conflicting goals, both of which are highly challenging.

First, as Nobel Laureate Dan Shechtman repeatedly urges, you *must become expert, truly expert, at something....* his expertise was in electron microscopy, and it enabled him to overcome fierce opposition to his discoveries, and ultimately win the big prize. You need deep knowledge in at least one field or subfield.

Second, you need to become curious and learn a great many things about a great many fields, not in depth but sufficient to understand them. You need wide knowledge, surface knowledge, in just about everything. Even if you have team members who have deep knowledge, it still helps a lot to innovate if you have basic understanding of other, distant disciplines.

---

[9] http://dc.mit.edu/sites/dc.mit.edu/files/MIT%20White%20Paper%20on%20Convergence.pdf

In future, all the major breakthroughs will occur at the point of convergence among several disciplines. In order for you, innovator, to be there, you need to acquire depth, and breadth.

Good luck!

Making "Eureka!" happen: On inviting "ah-hah" insights!

All of us have experienced a "Eureka!" moment — a sudden flash of insight that yields a creative solution to a problem. "Eureka!" is Greek for "I have found it!" allegedly shouted when Archimedes discovered his famous displacement principle.

Can you do things that make "ah-hah!" moments more frequent and more powerful? Apparently you can. In researching neuroscience for an upcoming conference, I found an article, *The Aha! Moment: The Cognitive Neuroscience of Insight*, by John Kounios (Drexel U.) and Mark Beeman (Northwestern U.). [Recent Directions in Neurological Science, 2009.]

The authors use EEG (electromagnetic imaging) and fMRI (functional MRI imaging) of the brain to physically map "Eureka!" moments. They give subjects a 'compound remote association' problem: e.g. find a single word that can form a compound word or familiar 2-word phrase with EACH of three words. E.g. crab, pine, sauce. One answer: "apple" (applesauce, crabapple, pineapple). They map brain patterns while subjects tackle the problem. They then ask the subjects to say whether the solution "popped into their minds" ("Eureka!") or resulted from analysis (e.g. 'cake'... crab cake, but pine cake no; reject cake; crabgrass ... no, apple grass doesn't work...etc.).

Here is what they, and others, have found: "Eureka!" problem-solving "can be influenced by the prior preparatory state". As Pasteur said, "chance favors the prepared mind." "Eureka!" comes to those who prepare for it. A relaxed, pleasant state of mind is far better for "Eureka!" than tension. (Attention, companies that put workers' feet to the fire to develop ideas.) Humor is very conducive to "Eureka!". And most important: "individuals high in creativity habitually deploy their attention in a diffuse rather than a focused manner". I.e. we get to "Eureka!", not in a straight linear line, but zigzag.

The authors believe you can organize "Eureka!"' thinking, as a 'cascade of processes' that generate "aha!" I agree. Zoom in! Think hard about a problem. Then let your mind wander. Soar into the clouds. Zoom out! Think of wild ideas that make you laugh. Bring a shopping cart with you, and dump all the possible ideas into it. At some point — pause. Zoom in again. Take your shopping cart and start to empty its contents. Choose one solution in it you think will work. Listen carefully to your gut. This could be a "Eureka!" Or "aha!" moment. If it is — listen to it! And then — get to work.

Why dreams make you happy...until they come true

The lovely blog called *Babbage,* on science and technology, in *The Economist,* wrote about a neat piece of behavioral research. It is by a team led by Eugene Caruso, University of Chicago, and will appear in *Psychological Science.*[10]

Here is the experiment: "323 volunteers [recruited through Mechanical Turk, Amazon's micro-job portal] were divided into two groups. For one group, a week before Valentine's Day (February 14), they were asked how they planned to celebrate it. A week after February 14, the second group reported how they HAD celebrated."

Both groups had to describe how near the day they felt, on a scale of one to seven.

Those describing future plans were far more likely to report it as "a short time from now". Those who already experienced it tended to report "a long time ago".

Conclusion: "Something happening in one month feels psychological closer than something that happened a month ago".

---

[10]http://www.economist.com/blogs/babbage/2013/04/psychology-time

CHAPTER SIX | Restoring Lost Innovativeness 129

Does this jibe with YOUR experience? Do you get much enjoyment out of anticipating future pleasures, like vacations, purchases, family events? Do past events, purchases, etc., somehow feel distant and perhaps a bit ho-hum?

Caruso speculates that depression may occur because people who feel the past as being closer may ruminate about the bad things that occurred to them. Babbage thinks politicians should talk more about future plans than about the past. (I think they already do this, but boringly.)

For individuals: Perhaps we should emulate the Japanese. Americans, when they buy something online, want it NOW! Japanese don't mind waiting two weeks, because they like to anticipate the purchase's arrival during the waiting period. It's pretty simple. Keep a host of pleasant future events lined up in your mind, and replenish the list from time to time; take the list out when you're a bit down, and go over it in your mind. Reap the sunshine it brings. Don't count on all the old stuff you bought to keep you happy; it fades quickly. Dreams themselves make us happy; once they come true, well — perhaps they fade a little. So — dream on!

Are your windows open? Are you sure?

This morning I took part in a superbly-organized charity run, in which runners earned money for charity by completing a 2-kilometer. route as many times as they can — about $5 went to the charity for each route completion. I did 6 kms. The route began at the Central Park in Upper Haifa, ran along the beautiful Promenade overlooking the sea, and circled back. Afterward, I went nearby for a haircut. The barber shop was perhaps 200 yards from the finish line. My barber asked me about my ID number, still pinned to my T-shirt. I told him about the run. He was unaware — despite the hubbub, crowds, noise, DJ's, etc. He just hadn't bothered to open his windows, or his eyes and ears.

I thought about how many of us keep our windows closed, figuratively. How many amazing things are going on in the world, but we are missing them, because our windows are closed? And we keep them closed, because to open them might let in wind and rain. But they might also let in, say, a shooting star.

So, how do we go about opening our windows? Talk to people. I wear unusual ties, just to start conversations. Give some change to a street musician or a homeless person. Talk to them. Ask them about their lives. Make eye contact with people and you might get a reaction.

So, are your windows open? Are you sure? If not — open them. You'll be amazed how much more fun life is. A chance encounter might just create a new friend, or even change your life. It's happened to me more than once.

A thousand "True Fans": YOU can do it!

By chance, I encountered a blog with a clever title and a powerful point: http://kk.org/thetechnium/1000-true-fans/ Here is the main point:

There are two places innovators look for ideas. One is the 'long tail' — esoteric niche markets, on the long largely-unoccupied tail of the normal curve. The density of users and buyers here is too low to support life, generally. The second is the fat middle, where ordinary people reside. Here, competition is fierce, advantages lie with incumbents and habit dominates (ever try to get people who love vanilla ice cream to try chocolate?).

The alternative suggests the author, is to find 1,000 "True Fans" (defined as people who will buy anything and everything you produce). Here is the calculation:

If a "True Fan" will spend one day's wages per year supporting what you do, that comes to: 1,000 × $100 equals $100,000. Presto — you have a business!

If you are patient, if you add one "True Fan" a day, it will only take you three years to build a real business. But, you have to maintain contact with your "True Fans". Web 2.0 and 3.0 enables that. And, the circle of "True

Fans" is surrounded by "Lesser Fans", who sometimes will buy what you sell.

You don't need a hit to survive, says the author. There is a place in the middle, not the fat middle, and not the long tail. An 'artist' can aim for this spot, but I will add: ON ONLY ONE CONDITION! Be sure you are passionate about the offering you are making to your "True Fans". If you are not, then you are doing it only for money, and that means YOU yourself are not a "True Fan", so you can't expect a thousand others to be one.

Bipolar issues: Is self-confidence or humility a better motivator?

If you are an innovator, is it better to be supremely confident, even arrogant? Or is it better to be humble, self-effacing, modest?

The answer is: Yes. There appears to be a bipolar aspect to the underlying psychological attitudes that drive innovation. This emerges from research on self-esteem, noted in David Brooks' recent *NYT* column, and led by psychologist David Schmidt, of Bradley University, in Peoria, Illinois. This research measures national self-esteem: *Confidence in our ability to think, to cope with the basic challenges of life and confidence in our right to be successful and happy.* His team measured self-esteem in a large number of countries.[11]

The top six are:

- Serbia: 33.59
- Chile: 33.12
- Israel: 33.03
- Peru: 33.01
- Estonia: 32.63
- United States: 32.21

---

[11] Miranda Hitti, *Who's No. 1 in Self-Esteem? Serbia Is Tops, Japan Ranks Lowest, U.S. Is No. 6 in Global Survey,* WebMD Health News, September 27, 2005.

Note that among these, Israel, Estonia and the U.S. are highly innovative nations, whose entrepreneurs are endowed with great self-confidence and willingness to undertake risk.

However, consider also the bottom-ranked nations, with Japan the lowest of all:

* Taiwan: 28.77
* Czech Republic: 28.47
* Bangladesh: 27.80
* Hong Kong: 27.54
* Japan: 25.50

Among these nations, Taiwan and Hong Kong are highly entrepreneurial and innovative. But Japan is not. Taiwan and Hong Kong appear to have entrepreneurial drive arising from 'worst-case scenarios' — bad things may happen, if they do you will have only yourself and your own wealth and savings to rely on. Japan's self-effacing culture of modesty and understatement does not seem to boost innovation.

In general, I believe that innovation is highly dependent on national culture, but each nation that excels in innovation does so, in its own way, unique and distinctive. This is why nations that have tried to emulate other nations' innovation ecosystems have generally failed. The message for nations that seek to become more innovate is: You can do it, either through supreme self-confidence, or utter lack of self-confidence and self-esteem — but you *can* do it.

The greatest innovation of all — your life, or — we can ALL be Bill Gates

In an amusing op-ed piece this morning in *The New York Times*,[12] Zick Rubin writes about how a psychology website wikia.com reported his

---

[12] Zick Rubin, *How the Internet tried to Kill Me*, The New York Times, March 12, 2011, http://www.nytimes.com/2011/03/13/opinion/13rubin.html?mtrref=www.google.co.il&gwh=B889B6955631969AE35E0885C92DA24A&gwt=pay&assetType=opinion

death ("Zick Rubin, 1944–1997") — prematurely, recalling Mark Twain's famous comment to a journalist "reports of my death are greatly exaggerated" (usually misstated as "...reports of my death are premature"). Rubin had to struggle to correct this. But what is most interesting is that Rubin writes of how he ended a great career as Harvard Psychology Professor and in midlife became a media lawyer! He was literally reborn.

The greatest innovation many of us will face is within our own lives. We will need to reinvent ourselves in midlife, at least once. But how? According to Strenger and Ruttenberg[13]: avoid two extremes. Myth One: "the myth that midlife marks the onset of decline". It doesn't. Your cumulative wisdom will far outweigh your physical decline. Myth Two: "the myth of magical transformation through vision and willpower". You probably cannot become a concert pianist, even if you do practice 20,000 hours.

Use the "adjacent possible". What do I know now that could be useful in a new but related activity ("adjacent to what I do now, but far enough to be interesting and challenging")? And what am I passionate about, to drive the energy I need for this transformation?

I know a great many successful managers and entrepreneurs who find new meaning in their second lives, through social activities — using their skills and wisdom to tackle social ills and problems, after building global companies and shaping world-changing innovations. Social entrepreneurship is 'adjacent', it is 'possible', but also new and challenging enough to energize. Bill Gates is an example. He is using his wealth and his foundation, along with organizational and innovative skills, to tackle such problems as malaria, child immunization and developing a TB vaccine.

Humble masterpieces: M&M's

Ever wonder how M&M's were invented? Paolo Antonelli has compiled a fine book about how many humble masterpieces, like M&M's, came into existence.[14]

---

[13]Carlo Strenger & Arie Ruttenberg, *The Existential Necessity of Midlife Change*, Harvard Business Review, February 2008.
[14]Paola Antonelli, *Humble Masterpieces: Everyday Marvels of Design*, Harper Collins: 2005.

Like many wonderful innovations, M&M's were not invented, but rather — discovered, observed and perfected.

An American named Forrest Mars (the M&M company is still named Mars, and is the largest confectionary company in the world; the other "M" is his partner, Bruce Murrie) visited Spain during the Spanish Civil War (1936–1939). He noticed that Spanish soldiers were eating chocolate covered with a hard sugary coating. The coating kept the chocolate from melting.

When he came home to America, Mars developed a recipe for M&M's. When WWII broke out, he made and sold M&M's to the US Army and soldiers fighting n Europe consumed large amounts of them. After the war, Mars began to market M&M's to the public, in cardboard tubes. Later, he shifted to the plastic packets we know today.

M&M's has stuck fast to its original look and product over the decades. It added chocolate-coated peanuts in 1954. Since then, Mars has added incremental innovations, such as new colors — pink, and blue.

A great many of the 'humble masterpieces' were built on sharp-eyed observations by innovators, rather than do-it-from-scratch inventions.

Innovators: Is your vision 20/20? Do you watch constantly for ways people use conventional products differently, to overcome constraints, to make their lives easier? Do you observe closely how people use your *own* products or services, in unusual ways? When the founders of Quicken (book-keeping software) saw that people were buying Quicken not to manage their checkbooks (its original intention) but actually to run their small businesses, they quickly moved to exploit this huge unexpected market.

This is why time to market is so crucial for innovations. Get it out there fast! Then observe and learn. Often this is the only way you will discover what the true market is for your product, and what its true Unique Value Proposition is, and for whom!

CHAPTER SEVEN

Learning Creativity from Our Kids

Introduction

Suppose, just suppose, that a *Creativity Olympics* was held every four years, just like the Summer and Winter Olympics. Suppose there were no age limits for competitors. Who would win all the gold medals?

The answer is: five-year-olds. Children aged five are super-geniuses in creativity, at least 98 percent of them are, according to research. The reason? They have not yet been told what is impossible. So everything is possible. Everything. Everything can become anything. They would easily defeat even high-IQ adults in an Olympic creativity event (such as, what things could you do with a fire truck, which is one of the simpler creativity tests; most adults find it hard to think of anything other than play with the truck as a truck). Then, we send our five-year-olds to school. At school, they are taught what is possible, taught the rules. And their creativity plummets, as will be shown in this chapter. Trillions of dollars of valuable human resources are destroyed, wantonly, at one stroke, all over the world, in schools where the ability to excel at test-taking is the goal rather than the ability to generate new ideas. But because the lost creativity does not have a true market value, the destruction, massive, is ignored.

Children are amazing. One way to restore lost adult creativity is to return to the playfulness of our childhood. Usually, adults teach children. In creativity, we adults have much to *learn* from our children. When schools reduce or eliminate playtime, they are doing enormous damage to children and to society. If organizations want to become more creative, they should consider introducing the adult equivalent of recess — unstructured open playtime, for fun, laughter, and relaxation. Because creativity flourishes in an atmosphere of fun and laughter — which is the last thing many organizations today are willing to tolerate, in a highly serious warlike atmosphere of global competition.

How teachers ruin inquiring minds — and why they must stop

Thanks to my outstanding colleagues at Technion's Center for Improvement of Teaching and Learning, our MOOC (massive open online course), *Cracking the Creativity Code: Part One — Discovering Ideas*, launched on the Coursera website on May 18, 2015 and has over 15,000 students enrolled, worldwide, from Qatar, India, China, Iran, Iraq and Saudi Arabia, among others. The course is based in part on the book by the same name by Ruttenberg & Maital.

Part of the course involves "chat" forums, organized as 'forums' on topics the students themselves initiate.

Lizzie writes: "My 7th grade teacher's response to many a question was 'don't show your ignorance by asking that', which didn't reduce my ignorance but did get me to stop asking questions and start hating school instead of loving it." Malgorzata responds: "Oh yes. I have suffered high school phobia because of it. Constant bullying by teachers was unbearable."

How many teachers encourage questions? How many shut them off, destroying the spirit of inquiry and love of learning? Are teacher training schools helping teachers encourage students' questions, rather than shutting them off?

Javier writes about how his teacher, in Barcelona, requires the students to copy verbatim a short story. He tried an experiment — writing with his eyes closed, to see if he could write straight lines without looking. The teacher ridiculed him before the class. End of experiment. Could the teacher have responded: "Class! Javier is trying to write with his eyes closed. Let's all try it. Let's see what happens. Javier, thank you for this interesting idea."

There are millions of superb, dedicated teachers all over the world, educating the next generation, overworked, underpaid, underappreciated. But there are still too many to believe they should be teaching the laws of algebra, rather than (in addition) why mathematics is interesting and fun to explore.

The Nobel Laureate in Physics, Isidore Rabi tells this story: When he came home from school, his mother never asked him, what did you learn today in school? Instead she asked, Isadore, did you ask good questions in class today? He attributes his success as a scientist to his mother and to her question. How many Nobel Prizes are we destroying, by shutting off kids' questions?

Internet of everything

In 1982, engineers at Carnegie Mellon University, in Pittsburgh, Pennsylvania, built a *Coke* machine connected to the Internet (or the existing network — Internet did not yet exist), that could report how many *Cokes* had been sold and how cold they were. This was perhaps the birth of what we know now as the *Internet of Everything* — everything, everyone, connected, everywhere, all the time, by the Internet. By 2025, only 10 years from now, some 25–50 billion devices will be connected — cars (self drive), fridges, people, computers, machines, virtually everything.

Great? A new 20 trillion dollar industry? Jobs? Happy people?

Perhaps. But the downside could be a sharp decline in people's social skills. And social skills, society, collaboration, community, friendship, helping others, this is what makes us human, what keeps the world more or less together.

Writing in *The New York Times*, Claire Cain Miller makes a key point: "Occupations that require strong social skills have grown much more than others since 1980". Yet cultivating those social skills is on the decline, in schools focused on homework and tests. Increasingly, worldwide, even kindergarten kids are getting homework, instead of time to play.

We recently visited Touchstone Community School in Grafton, MA. We spoke with Cheryl and Tamara, who teach young children. We shared recess with the kids, and romped in big grassy fields, threw Frisbees and learned to do cartwheels. We saw how vital recesses, and play, are, for young children. And above all, we saw how easily very young children related to us, strangers, called us by first names (a Touchstone touchstone), asked how we are, what we are doing, and even interviewed us. Those social skills did not just happen. They were cultivated. And they grew especially in playtime, in recess. We saw an older boy play with a wheel device, and a small child stood in front of it. The natural instinct: shove him aside. What the boy did? Gently put his hand on the small child's shoulder, explained to him that he was in the way, and asked him if he would please move aside. THAT is a social skill. Perhaps as important as knowing 8 times 9 is 72.

Technical skills can be automated, the author notes. But social skills? We have to learn them, make them a part of our social DNA from an early age. Pre-kindergarten is crucial for this. We must do everything to preserve the 'soft' skills learned in school, because they are the ones that are 'hard' to acquire later, and make us employable.

Touchstone School — magical moments

My wife and I visited Touchstone Community School, in Grafton, MA, about an hour from Boston. I would like to recount briefly some "magical moments" I experienced there, in a pre-K to Grade 8 school where children do not take formal tests and where their imaginations and social skills are fostered.

Background: Thanks to the hospitality of Touchstone, I've brought a Chinese family from Shantou, Guangdong (where Technion has a joint venture program), to visit the school — Jin, my former Shantou University student, his wife Yuen, and 3-year-old daughter Yue, or Sophia. Together we're making a documentary film, hoping to bring the message of Touchstone's "transformative schooling" back to China and to Israel.

Values: We joined a group of Grade 7–8 children discussing Touchstone core values. The class itself had earlier chosen core values: all began with "c" — confidence, curiosity, connection, creativity. These values appeared on a "flag" created by the children which included one square per child, where the square reflected the child's own personality. This emphasis at Touchstone on being an individual is pervasive.

I asked the students about rules. If you have core values, and act on them, do you really need rules? Rules are external, externally enforced; values are internal, internally enforced. The discussion was interesting, the consensus was — values can replace rules.

There followed a discussion about table arrangements. Pairs? Fours? One big square table? The consensus was: one big table, more inclusive. Inclusiveness is a school-wide core value. I suggested maybe an oval or round table? But there is no such table at Touchstone. However, there is an oval carpet. Let's sit around the carpet, the students suggested. I came up with a round table that splits into four segments, so work in pairs and small teams can take place. We need to have it built.

One conversation at a time? This is an IDEO principle. It is implemented in this class with *Jupiter*, a soft toy, tossed from one child (the speaker) to another (who raises their hands and wishes to speak). One child was applauded, for actually catching *Jupiter* with one hand (apparently, a first! The students joked about it...not in a mocking manner).

I could not help but notice the huge developmental gap between the girls and the boys … the girls are way ahead of the boys, which is common at this age.

There is a core issue here. Teachers who graduate from teachers' colleges learn about the rules of pedagogy and the rules of schooling. They then implement those rules in the schools where they teach, and children learn about following an external set of rules, with punishments (and rewards, at times). Children, who follow rules well, do well in school. Rebellious kids don't. But creativity demands rebellion. Are we eradicating it with our rule-based system? Touchstone begins with values. Values are internal. Why not replace external rules with internal values? And make "confidence", and "creativity" core values?

Kids of all ages (up to 100) need to play!

Hilary G. Conklin, Ph.D., is a fellow with the *OpEd Project* and an Associate Professor in the College of Education at DePaul University in Chicago. Writing in *TIME* magazine's *IDEAS* online blog, she writes: "Helicopter parents and teachers, stand down. Kids of all ages need time to learn through play in school." It's time we got serious about the crucial importance of play.

She continues: *"In classrooms across the country, the countdown to summer vacation has begun. The winter doldrums have always taken a toll, but in the era of test-dominated schooling and the controversial Common Core, it seems increasingly that it's not until summer that teenagers have any prospect for having fun anymore. One of the casualties of current education reform efforts has been the erosion of play, creativity, and joy from teenagers' classrooms and lives, with devastating effects. Researchers have documented a rise in mental health problems — such as anxiety and depression — among young people that has paralleled a decline in children's opportunities to play. And while play has gotten deserved press in recent months for its role in fostering crucial social-emotional and cognitive skills and cultivating creativity and imagination in the early childhood years, a critical group has been largely left out of these important conversations. Adolescents, too — not to mention adults, as shown through Google's efforts — need time to play, and they need time to play in school early childhood educators have known about and capitalized on the learning and developmental benefits of play for ages."*

"To be sure," she continues, *"there are times to be serious in school. The complex study of genocide or racism in social studies classrooms, for example, warrant students' thoughtful, ethical engagement, while crafting an evidence-based argument in support of a public policy calls upon another set of student skills and understandings. As with all good teaching, teachers must be deliberate about their aims. But, given that play allows for particular kinds of valuable learning and development, there should be room in school to cultivate all of these dimensions of adolescent potential. Purposefully infusing play into middle and high school classrooms holds the potential for a more joyful, creative, and educative future for us all — a future in which kids have more interesting."*

Dr. Conklin might have added that adults, too, of all ages, especially us senior citizens, need opportunities to fool around, imagine, create and play. Creative ideas emerge from an ambience of fun, joking and just general fooling around.

KidZania: Where kids find reality, not fantasy

"We make people happy." This is *Disney's* famous mantra, implemented to perfection at *Disney* theme parks in California, Florida, Hong Kong, suburban Paris and elsewhere.

"We make kids grown-ups". This could be the mantra of *KidZania*, a worldwide chain of theme parks where kids aged four to 14 get the chance to enact the roles of grownups in lavish, scaled-down worlds. The story of *KidZania* is told in Rebecca Mead's article in the latest *New York Times* magazine (*When I Grow Up*, January 19, 2015).

In *KidZania*, Mead explains, children "can work on a car assembly line, or move furniture, or put out fake fire with real water. *KidZania* has its own currency, *kidzos*, which can be used in branches around the world, or deposited and accessed with a realistic looking debit card." Children get a check for 50 *kidzos* on arrival and can add to it with a "salary" they earn for working. The most popular jobs (e.g. training to be a pilot on a flight simulator) pay less than the less popular ones, like being a dentist. (Kids look into a dummy's mouth — wonder how many kids pick THAT one!) Kids can rent a car (small electric go-karts) and buy stuff at the mini city's department store.

KidZania has its own language. "Kai!" means hi, along with placing two fingers over the heart. "Zanks" means thanks. By is "Z-U", from Santiago to Seoul. Adult staff are "Zupervisors". Staff ends conversations with kids by saying "have a productive day".

The founder is an entrepreneur, aged 50, named Xavier Lopez Ancona. His headquarters are near the *KidZania* in Centro Santa Fe mall, Mexico, one of Latin America's biggest shopping malls. *KidZania* now exists in over a dozen countries, including Japan, Malaysia, and Turkey. Lopez went to bizschool at Northwestern University and ran GE's private equity business in Mexico. A friend in the toy importing business came to him with an idea for a role-playing park for kids. Lopez joined the venture. The Santa Fe Park opened in September 1999. In the first year, 800,000 people came to it, double what the founders expected.

Lopez is careful to vary the *KidZania* parks according to the venue. In Mexico kids spend their *kidzos* as soon as they get them. In Japan it is hard to persuade kids to part with their *kidzos* for any reason. In Lisbon kids come with their parents. In the Gulf States kids come with nannies or are dropped off by their drivers. In *KidZania* in Jeddah, Saudi Arabia, girls will be allowed to drive cars — a privilege their moms don't have and hence definitely, in my opinion, subversive.

Mead quotes one child in Kuwait: "In Kuwait parents and adults have responsibility for everything you do. In *KidZania* it is different — it's like kids rule the world. That's fun, but you can also learn how hard and complicated it is and how adults feel when they work. I have learned that being an adult is actually hard."

WIX: Playfulness & innovation

I have the privilege of visiting startups and writing about them. Yesterday I visited *WIX*, an Israeli company which, with over 60 million users, leads the world in services for building beautiful websites. It is the first such company that has done an IPO (on NASDAQ). It is based in North Tel Aviv.

The first thing I notice at such startups is the physical ambience. *WIX* chose to locate not in Tel Aviv's high-tech area, in North Tel Aviv, but near Tel Aviv Port, which is a playground for thirty-somethings. The reception desk is the first thing you notice. It conveys playfulness. This is crucial. *WIX* is not a startup but is in the scale-up stage. It has strong revenues and a gross profit margin of over 80 percent. But it retains its atmosphere of creativity and playfulness. You encounter this from the outset, when you check in at the reception desk.

In its crowded building on Namal St., it has a rooftop area with a stunning view of the Mediterranean, where social gatherings are held. Like *Google's* Mountainview campus, food is readily available, and coffee. *WIX* employs 800 people, 600 of whom are based in Israel; but despite its size, it tries to retain the feeling of being small, lively and playful.

Recently at a seminar at Tel Aviv University, participants told me about the difference between "play", "playing", and "playfulness". The latter is a kind of mindset that nearly always disappears in large organizations, when manuals, handbooks, protocols and procedures are set up. *WIX* has so far retained it. I hope it will continue to do so.

Can you come out to play? *Will* you?

I'm married to a very smart psychologist, who is an expert on children and play; as a result, I get to read many interesting, sometimes wonderful, articles. The latest is one published in 2007, by L.A. Barnett, titled *The nature of playfulness in young adults*.[1] The purpose of the article was to see if the term "playfulness" could become a valid "construct", i.e. a clear, well-defined concept recognizable by all and useful for further research. To this end, the author used focus groups of adults.

The result: A rather long, but insightful, definition of "playfulness" in adults.

Here it is. Read it. See if you have these qualities. Why? Because, as the author notes, "playful people are uniquely able to transform virtually any environment to make it more stimulating, enjoyable and entertaining." An extreme example: Roberto Benigni's *Life is Beautiful*, a film about a father who made life in a Nazi concentration camp into a game, for his young son (Academy Award, Best Actor 1999).

Playfulness is the predisposition to frame (or reframe) a situation in such a way as to provide oneself (and possibly others) with amusement, humor and/or entertainment. Individuals who have such a heightened predisposition are typically funny, humorous, spontaneous, unpredictable, impulsive, active, energetic, adventurous, sociable, outgoing, cheerful, and happy, and are likely to manifest playful behavior by joking, teasing, clowning, and acting silly.

---

[1] L.A. Barnett, *The Nature of Playfulness in Young Adults*, Personality and Individual Differences, 43 (2007), pp. 949–958.

Do any of those adjectives describe you? Yes? No? If no — do you want them to? If so, you can definitely change. Just remember how you played when you were a child, and copy yourself as you once were.

What does this have to do with innovation? "Reframing" (seeing the same thing differently from others) is a key part of playfulness, and a key aspect of creativity. If you can "reframe" to play, you can "reframe" to create.

The three biggest ideas in history — and the biggest of all

I'm reading a big thick book, Peter Watson's book *Ideas: a history of thought and invention, from fire to Freud*, [Harper Perennial, 2006], over 800 pages, and 75 pages of close endnotes.

Let me try to summarize it for you, though I recommend that you try to plough through it.

Watson says that the three most influential ideas in history (only a very brave person would assert he could identify the three BIGGIES!) are:

1. The soul.
2. The idea of Europe.
3. The experiment.

Now, Watson does not say this, but two of his big ideas have really not worked out too well. The soul? Well, this idea is a foundation of religion. And religion has caused death, wars, suffering, persecution, and continues to do so (see ISIS, Hamas, and other fundamentalists).

Europe? Well, Europe has ended wars within Europe, especially between France and Germany. But by placing monetary union ahead of political union, Europe put the cart before the horse, and horses are very poor at pushing carts, though good at pulling them. There is a good chance England may opt out of Europe, and that will be a severe blow.

But the experiment? Now THERE is an idea. How do you learn about the world? Well, you can pretend you know. But as Goethe said, thinking is better than knowing, but looking is best of all. So, you learn about the world by trying experiments. If you're a scientist, you have a lab and you can do controlled experiments. If you're a social scientist, you let the world be your lab and watch closely for natural experiments — places where unusual things happen — and learn from them. If you're an entrepreneur, by definition you are an experimentalist. Your product is by definition an experiment. The only way you will learn if it truly creates value, is by getting it out into the marketplace, and have people use it.

So, Peter Watson, you got one right out of three. We all should become experimenters. This is a mindset. Don't be afraid to try things. Don't be afraid to fail (most experiments fail). See my previous blog. And become an experimenter in your daily life as well. Try new foods, music, books, magazines, TV programs … welcome experiments, even though they may be uncomfortable. (The old familiar stuff is comfortable; the new unfamiliar stuff is Uncomfortable.) Soon, you will become more comfortable with experiments. And the mindset will spread to your work as entrepreneur and innovator.

Destroying our most precious resource — and it's not air or water

In an interview for the *AARP* (retired persons) magazine, Warren Buffett warns against investing in gold, and in doing so, informs us how much gold there is in the world: 170,000 tons, which if melted together would form a cube 68 feet on each side, worth $9.6 trillion (at $1,750 per ounce). Wow…that's a lot of cash, more than half America's annual GDP.

Now — imagine reverse alchemy: irradiating that cube until it becomes … lead. $10 trillion in value disappears instantly. Gone forever.

Insanity? We are doing the equivalent every day to our children.

Studies show that nearly all (98 percent) 3-to-5 year-olds score as creative geniuses, when measured by their divergent thinking skills (ability to envision multiple solutions to a problem — matching the definition of creativity as 'widening the range of choices'). [The test is used by NASA to measure creativity among its employees.] By age 10, only 32 percent scored at genius level. By age 15, 10 percent. And by adulthood: 2 percent![2] [see figure 7.1].

---

[2]George Land & Beth Jarman, *Breakpoint and Beyond: Mastering the Future — Today*, Leadership 2000 Inc, August 1, 1998.

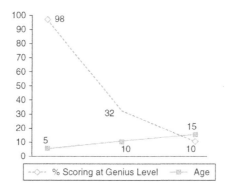

Figure 7.1   Decline of ceativity by age.
Source: Land & Jarman, 1992.

We can only blame the way kids learn in schools for this. Rigid, regimented, this-is-the-right-way convergent thinking, my way or the highway.

What is the value of this destroyed creativity? Far far more than that cube of gold. Imagine all the wonderful ideas we will never have, to enrich our lives and change the world, because our young geniuses have their creative sparks extinguished. And we can never get it back.

If only there was awareness of the problem. If only we could stop destroying creativity in our children, by a few simple ways to foster divergent thinking.

Is anyone listening?

Education researcher Y. Zhao notes, in a 2009 book: "In their 1998 book *Breakpoint and Beyond: Mastering the Future — Today*, Land and Jarman (1998)[3] describe a longitudinal study on creativity beginning in the 1960s. Land administered eight tests of divergent thinking, which measure an individual's ability to envision multiple solutions to a problem. NASA uses these tests to measure the potential for creative work by its employees. When the tests were first given to 1,600 three- to five- year-olds, *Land found 98 percent of them to score at a level called creative genius. But five years later when the same group of children took the tests, only 32 percent scored at this level and after another five years, the percentage of geniuses declined to 10 percent.* Figure 0.1 illustrates the sharp decline in one measure of creativity as children get older. By 1992, more than 200,000 adults had taken the same tests and only 2 percent scored at the genius level."

---

[3] Ibid.

Falling creativity: Not just kids

With so many bad things happening in the world today, it seems rather strange to be so worried about the decline of creativity. But I am. I work with talented managers who consistently report that their ideas are unwelcome in their organizations. And I observe lock-step linear schools that seem obsessed by erasing any shred of independent thinking among their children.

The reason declining creativity should worry us so much is this: The magnitude and number of problems in the world today are growing; but the resources to deal with them are shrinking. (It's called 'austerity'.) So the only way we are going to make a difference and change the world is through creativity — creating something from nothing, widening the range of choices without using resources. But if creativity itself is being degraded — we are in deep trouble.

Here is the essence of an interview found on *Britannica* website with Kyung Hee Kim, a professor at College of William & Mary in Williamsburg, Va., a scholar whose research revealed the depth and extent of falling creativity.[4]

* Children in the U.S., especially those in kindergarten through third grade, are becoming less creative (measured by the widely accepted TTCT Torrance Tests of Creative Thinking). There is no real explanation for this yet.
* For kids: Prof. Kyung thinks the cause may be in their homes, not in their schools; kids spend most of their time in front of TV, computers, video games, and far less time engaged in creative activities and play.
* Kids are spending far more time interfacing with machines, rather than with people and paper.

---

[4]http://blogs.britannica.com/2010/10/the-decline-of-creativity-in-the-united-states-5-questions-for-educational-psychologist-kyung-hee-kim

* Video games are a growing part of kids' play. Prof. Kyung does not believe playing video games fosters creativity. Creativity is widening the range of choices. But video games are programmed and offer limited choices.
* "Contemporary parenting styles" may create overly programmed lives for children, over-protecting them and denying them opportunities to discover for themselves.
* Dramatic increases in ADHD diagnoses and over-prescription of medication necessarily "decrease creativity, as creative kids and ADHD kids share common characteristics: rebellious, emotionally expressive, spontaneous, impulsive, energetic, excitable kids." "We are unwittingly doping our creative children in a misguided attempt to control undesirable and inconvenient behaviors!"
* Creativity scores are falling because "society is less receptive and encouraging of creativity, creative people, creative ideas."

I myself frequently encounter companies that pay lip service to innovation but do everything they can to destroy any wayward, creative disruptive new idea.

* *No Child Left Behind Act* (NCLB) has teachers teaching to an annual test in reading and math, "which discourages purposeful creativity development".

Prof. Kyung concludes, disturbingly: ".... countries such as China, Japan, Korea, and Taiwan have modeled their educational systems after the earlier American education system because of America's previous success in encouraging creativity in children. Ironically, in the U.S., NCLB now mandates standardized testing and national educational standards, fosters rote memorization, and chokes creativity in children."

Kids' creativity is declining: Is "No Child Left Behind" responsible?

Can you test for creativity and measure it, like IQ, in individuals — especially kids? Dr. E. Paul Torrance[5] developed the TTCT, *Torrance Tests for Creative Thinking*, in 1957. It is a fairly simple 90-minute set of tasks, extended in 1966. His tests have five activities: ask-and-guess, product improvement, unusual uses, unusual questions and "just suppose". One task gives children a toy fire truck and asks them how they would improve it. One of his subjects, in 1958, found 25 different ways! Torrance used his TTCT to show that you CAN teach creativity.

---

[5] Paul E Torrance, *Teaching for creativity*, Journal of Creative Behavior, 6, 114–143, 1972.

Recently, strong evidence was found to support the premise that *IQ and creativity are almost unrelated*. Back in 1958, Prof. Torrance tested the creativity of a group of 400 Minneapolis children. In the 55 years since then, Torrance and his colleague Garnet Millar tracked the children, recording their patents, businesses, research papers, grants, books, art exhibits, software programs, ad campaigns — virtually everything. In turns out that *Torrance's creativity index predicted the children's creative accomplishments as adults incredibly accurately*. The correlation between lifetime creative accomplishment and childhood creativity is more than three times higher than the correlation between accomplishment and childhood IQ.

What's even more interesting, and worrisome, is this: According to the "Flynn effect", named after New Zealand Prof. James Flynn, with each generation, IQ goes up by 10 points. With creativity, a reverse trend was identified. American creativity scores are falling, according to researcher Kyung Hee Kim. "The decrease is very significant," Kim says. He notes it is the scores of younger children in America, from kindergarten to sixth grade, for whom the decline is most serious.

In 2000, just after he was elected (or in fact, lost the election and then stole it thanks to Florida's Republican State Supreme Court), George Bush pushed through the NCLB (*No Child Left Behind Act*). While NCLB focuses on measuring and improving conventional learning skills, creativity is suffering. One wonders whether rule-based education, in which teachers teach kids to pass tests, is actually hurting break-the-rules creativity, even in innately creative young children. If this is so, there is cause for concern. America needs engineers who know how to make things others invent — but it also needs those who know how to invent things others will make. *Surely we can figure out how to teach both, without ruining either.*

The Creativity Crisis, July 10, 2010, Po Bronson & Ashley Merryman, *The Daily Beast* (*Newsweek*).

Kids continue to amaze: Ethiopian children master tablets

A recent article in *MIT Technology Review* reports on how the *One Laptop Per Child* project, led by Nicholas Negroponte, has morphed into the *One Tablet*

Per Child — and how children in a remote Ethiopian village, with no access to schooling, have conquered tablet computers with preloaded programs in English with exceptional speed! They even hacked the tablets and enabled disabled cameras!

The devices involved are Motorola Xoom tablets — used together with a solar charging system, which OLPC workers had taught adults in the village to use. Once a week, an OLPC worker visits the villages and swaps out memory cards so that researchers can study how the machines were actually used. After several months, the kids in both villages were still heavily engaged in using and recharging the machines, and had been observed reciting the "alphabet song," and even spelling words. One boy, exposed to literacy games with animal pictures, opened up a paint program and wrote the word "Lion."

The experiment is being done in two isolated rural villages with about 20 first-grade-aged children each, about 50 miles from Addis Ababa. One village is called Wonchi, on the rim of a volcanic crater at 11,000 feet; the other is called Wolonchete, in the Rift Valley. Children there had never previously seen printed materials, road signs, or even packaging that had words on them, Negroponte said. Earlier this year, OLPC workers dropped off closed boxes containing the tablets, taped shut, with no instruction. "I thought the kids would play with the boxes. Within four minutes, one kid not only opened the box, found the on-off switch ... powered it up. Within five days, they were using 47 apps per child, per day. Within two weeks, they were singing *ABC* songs in the village, and within five months, they had hacked *Android*," Negroponte said. "Some idiot in our organization or in the Media Lab had disabled the camera, and they figured out the camera, and had hacked Android."

Elaborating later on Negroponte's hacking comment, Ed McNierney, OLPC's chief technology officer, said that the kids had gotten around OLPC's effort to freeze desktop settings. "The kids had completely customized the desktop — so every kid's tablet looked different. We had installed software to prevent them from doing that," McNierney said. "And the fact they worked around it was clearly the kind of creativity, the kind of inquiry, the kind of discovery that we think is essential to learning." "If they can learn to read, then they can read to learn."

Giving computers directly to poor kids without any instruction is even more ambitious than OLPC's earlier pushes. "What can we do for these 100 million kids around the world who don't go to school?" McNierney said. "Can we give them a tool to read and learn — without having to provide schools and teachers and textbooks and all that?"

Kids are more creative than ever — some adults, less!

There is empirical evidence that our kids are more creative now than kids were, 25 years ago. (Alas, I have a strong feeling; we adults are LESS creative, especially those of us working in large bureaucratic organizations, which is nearly all of us.)

Here is the evidence. *Case Western Reserve* researchers Sandra Russ and her student Jessica Dillon compared 14 studies of child creativity, done in Russ' lab between 1985 and 2008. Each study used the same scale to evaluate children's cognition and emotional expression during five minutes of unstructured play.[6] Here is the method:

Affect in Play Scale: (APS): Each child was met with individually and given two neutral-looking puppets and three blocks with which to play however he or she would like. The task is appropriate for children ages 6–10, in grades 1–4. The play was videotaped and scored according to criteria in a scoring manual. The APS is relatively unstructured so that there is room for the child to structure the play and present affect themes that are habitual to him or her. The instructions for the task are: I am here to learn about how children play. I have here 2 puppets and would like you to play with them any way you like for 5 minutes. For example, you can have the puppets do something together. I also have some blocks that you can use. Be sure to have the puppets talk out loud. The video camera will be on so that I can remember what you say and do. I will tell you when to stop. Go ahead.[7]

---

[6]Sandra W. Russ and Jessica A. Dillon, *Changes in Children's Pretend Play Over Two Decades*, Case Western Reserve University, Creativity Research Journal, 23(4), 330 — 338, 2011.

[7]Scoring: The APS measures pretend play ability with five scores: 1. Organization rates the child's play (1–5) on the quality and complexity of the plot, considering cause and effect and plot integration. 2. Imagination rates the child's play (1–5) on its fantasy elements, block transformations, and number of novel ideas, characters, or events. 3. Comfort is a rating (1–5) of the child's comfort, involvement in the play and enjoyment of the play. 4. Frequency of Affect is a tally count of the number of units of verbal and non-verbal emotion expressed during the play. A unit is defined as one expression by an individual puppet that can be scored. For example, every time one puppet said, "I like you" or "I hate this" a unit is coded. The

According to the APA Monitor: "The researchers found that over the 23-year stretch, children's comfort and imagination scores improved, their organization and emotional expression numbers stayed the same, and their use of negative imagery decreased. According to Russ, the increase in imagination underscores children's resilience. "They are finding other ways to develop their imaginative abilities". Perhaps, she suggests, kids are being deprived of time to play freely, with more of their time being structured, so when they are allowed to let their imaginations run wild, they "take more advantage of it".

I think there are two main lessons here. First, let our kids have far more unstructured play time, to exercise their imaginations. Second, let us adults ALSO have more unstructured play time, idle time, time to let our imaginations roam free. If kids are creative, and adults aren't, perhaps we adults should be more like our kids. Simple, no?

*

Are we crippling our kids 'creativity'? The dilemma and a solution

Everybody knows the most creative nation in the world is the nation of five-year-olds. Small children have not yet learned the "rules", what is possible and real, and what is not. So in their world, everything is real, everything is possible. As a result, their imaginations run wild. Then we send them to Grade One — and methodically we stamp out their imaginative powers. And we buy them games and toys and show them TV shows

total number of units expressed during the 5-minute period is the frequency of affect score. Frequency of positive affect units and negative affect units are also obtained. 5. Variety of Affect is a tally count of the number of affect categories that are expressed during the play, drawing from 11 categories: Anger = Aggression, Anxiety = Fear, Happiness = Pleasure, Frustration = Dislike = Disappointment, Sadness = Hurt, Oral, Oral Aggression, Anal, Competition, Sexual, and Nurturance = Affection. These categories can be combined into positive affect expressions and negative affect expressions.

and movies where everything is incredibly real, in each detail, leaving no room for the imagination.

Here is what one of my blog readers, Anne Marie, from Singapore, notes about her own childhood:

I actually grew up in the Philippines, and growing up with just the basics, as a child I didn't have the privilege to have so many toys and technology before in a third world country is not even starting. But I am glad I did (and not even spoiled by my parents with all these toys) — it is because, I could clearly recall that I was only given a ball, a stick and some elastic bands, and from these three I was able to create hundreds of games with my playmates. I remember my childhood was so much fun. Now, I can see my nieces and nephews stuck in their computers, playing in a virtual world, but not an ounce of creativity at all! I sometimes shut their computers to test, and give them the basics … but how very minimum is the number of games that they can think of! But I am not giving up. A young mind is easier to train, so we will wait and see....

Thanks Anne Marie! There is a solution. Purposefully choose your children's toys and games and spare-time activities, to foster imagination. There are still many such games available. If you wish, make your own toys, out of cardboard and paper and sticks. Challenge them to create things, rather than prefer things that are already created. And when your child comes home and says he or she solves an arithmetic problem in an unusual way, and got a big red X on it from a rigid teacher — tear a strip off the teacher and the teacher's principal, and tell them about why you think children should be encouraged to be creative, rather than have their creativity doused by thoughtless in-the-box taskmasters.

It is not inevitable that kids should lose their creativity in school. This process can be stopped. But to do so is not easy. Take up your responsibility as a parent, and spring into action, before it is too late.

CHAPTER EIGHT

Innovating for Those with Less

Introduction

One of the principles of entrepreneurship is market size — innovate in markets that make such innovation worthwhile. In other words — find people with money, who can pay a lot for your creativity. But what about the two billion or so people in the world who are poor, and who do not have money? Are they to be ignored? Is creativity irrelevant for their needs?

The late strategy expert C.K. Prahalad wrote a wonderful book titled *The Fortune at the Bottom of the Pyramid*,[1] which became an acronym, FABP, for an approach to innovation that focused on low-cost innovations that served markets that were large in size, because millions of people had their needs met by these innovations priced for their pockets — when revenue is $P \times Q$, price times quantity, and even if P, price, is low, if Q, the number of those buying, is very large, the market can indeed be large. This is the bottom of the pyramid. It has been seriously ignored by innovators. And,

---

[1]C. K. Prahalad, *The Fortune at the Bottom of the Pyramid*, Wharton, University of Pennsylvania: Philadelphia, PA, 2004.

noted Prahalad, there are 4 billion people in the world, out of 7.5 billion, who have annual incomes less than $1,500.

This chapter features stories about creative people who sought to meet needs of those at the bottom of the pyramid. If your goal in life is, in Guy Kawasaki's words, to "make meaning", rather than just "make money", nothing can be more satisfying than innovating for those at the bottom of the pyramid, who in many ways deserve to be much closer to the top.

Rethinking innovation: Start at the bottom, not the top

Sometimes, rarely, you find pearls in advertising supplements.

The International New York Times' "Dawn of the New Decade" ad insert seeking investment in Asia (as if Asia needs money and investment, rather than the overspending America) has an interesting interview with Anil Gupta, INSEAD Professor and an expert on globalization.[2]

Here is Gupta's 'take' on the changing world of innovation:

"Enterprises that hope to emerge as the global leaders in 2020 will also need to think differently about innovation. Traditionally, innovation has originated in the developed countries .... within industries, at the top of a product range, for example, a Lexus, and then worked its way down to, say, a Toyota Corolla ... In order to capture the very large market opportunities in the low-to-middle segments [in emerging markets], the leading global enterprise of 2020 will need to be good at not just top-down innovation but also at frugal innovation, whose roots would lie in the low- and middle-income markets of emerging economies."

Prof. Gupta cites as an example Tata Group's *Nano* car, the world's cheapest, and its strategic plan to bring out an electric *Nano* in the EU and U.S., matching the performance of domestic equivalents at 1/3 less cost. "We'll see this phenomenon in many industries, from tractors to banking," he notes.

---

[2] *Emerging economies change the game for global corporations*, Dawn of the New Decade , Global New York Times, Friday August 27, 2010.

Innovator: Can you shift your focus from premium-priced 'toys' bought by those with scads of money, to low-priced products that even low-income groups in low-income countries can buy? The late C.K. Prahalad identified "fortunes at the bottom of the pyramid"… but apparently, according to Gupta, there are also superior innovation opportunities down there.

Two million women suffer — who cares? The terrible shame of fistula

If two million American, French, British or German women suffered from a life-destroying humiliating and unbearable condition — how many thousands of innovators and billions of R&D dollars would be devoted to finding a rapid solution?

But, fear not, it is only African, Asian and Arab women. So, who cares?

The condition is fistula. It is horrendous just to read about it. And despite a global campaign launched by that powerful, effective and efficient body called the United Nations, little progress has been made. We have excuses rather than results. It is a true disgrace, and a dark blot on the alleged human kindness of the wealthy half of the world.

The cost of curing the 2 million African, Asian and Arab women who suffer from the condition is $600 million, or $300 per woman, a sum equal to about *12 hours' worth of crude oil production*, or 0.1 percent of what the world spends annually on advertising.

According to the UN:

Obstetric fistula is a *hole in the birth canal caused by prolonged labor without prompt medical intervention, usually a Caesarean section.* The woman is left with chronic incontinence and, in most cases, a stillborn baby. *The smell of leaking urine or faeces, or both, is constant and humiliating, often driving loved ones away.* Left untreated, fistula can lead to chronic medical problems, including ulcerations, kidney disease, and nerve damage in the legs. *A simple surgery can normally repair the injury, with success rates as high as 90 percent for experienced surgeons. The average cost of fistula treatment and post-operative* *care is just US $300.* Sadly, most women with the condition do not know that treatment is available, or they cannot afford it. Like maternal mortality, fistula is almost entirely preventable. *But at least 2 million women in Africa, Asia and the Arab region are living with the condition*, and some 50,000–100,000 new cases develop each year. The persistence of fistula is a signal that health systems are failing to meet the needs of women.

If philanthropy is absent, where is creativity — a cheap effective solution poor women can afford? Where are the world's creative gynecologists? What about a mass-production "assembly line" surgical unit, portable, that can do hundreds of such operations, for example? What about enlisting 3,000 gynecologists and surgeons to donate a month a year curing fistula?

In 2003, UNFPA spearheaded the global *Campaign to End Fistula*, "a collaborative initiative to prevent fistula and restore the health and dignity of those living with its consequences." What a relief. Rather — what a joke.

Perhaps we need a campaign to end the *Campaign to End Fistula*, and get down to some real action. I don't see how we wealthy people sleep at night when so many people are suffering so badly, and so needlessly.

How strong minds raced so weak legs could walk

A U.S. National Football League charity campaign once used the slogan, "strong legs run so weak ones can walk". I recalled this during a visit yesterday to an Israeli startup named *Argo*, launched by Dr. Amit Goffer. *Argo's* product is called *ReWalk*, and it is an exoskeleton (outside-the-body skeleton) which, with electronics, enables those who cannot walk to stand on their own two feet and walk at 2 kilometer. per hour, a good clip. *ReWalk* can also enable people to climb stairs. You might call it, "strong minds race so that weak legs may walk".

Dr. Goffer told us that following a terrible accident, which left him paralyzed and confined to a wheelchair, he asked an audacious question: How can I create a device that enables people who cannot walk, to walk by themselves? Dr. Goffer has three degrees in electrical engineering, and worked for years at Odin Medical Technologies, which he started (real-time MRI images for brain surgery) and at Elscint (medical imaging). In 1998/9 he conceived of *ReWalk* and built a prototype himself. He described his approach to entrepreneurship: "not succeeding is not in my vocabulary. You create a corridor … you see a light at the end of it, and there are no exits, once you start you have to go all the way to the end, until you succeed."

Goffer estimates there are 2 million persons in the U.S. alone who are in wheelchairs, and of them, some 500,000 could use *ReWalk*. He is marketing the device to U.S. Rehabilitation Hospitals, including the Veterans' Administration. There are two models: one for institutions, like hospitals, and the other, for purchase by individuals. *Argo* has venture funding and employs 15 people in Israel, one in Europe and four in the U.S. It has several patents.

We saw a demonstration of *ReWalk*. Attached to a disabled person's legs, it uses an electronic sensor device on the person's wrist to move each leg forward, when the person (on crutches) leans forward. The battery power is carried in a small backpack. The device makes a whirring noise that is not unpleasant or loud. The price is currently $90,000 per device, in the U.S., and 90,000 Euros in Europe. This price will decline as large-scale manufacturing occurs. It finds use both as a 'walker' and as a rehabilitation device to help those who have been injured. By putting those confined to wheelchairs on their feet, erect, it essentially moves them from 'disabled' to 'enabled'. Goffer himself cannot use his device, as he is quadriplegic. But he nonetheless wants to get his device to market quickly. I told him I thought a great many people are waiting for it. "I know," he said. This is why he and his team are working very hard. Production currently takes place at the company's offices in Yokneam, a northern suburb of Haifa.

Check out www.argomedtec.com; this device is quite amazing.

Value from old truck tarpaulins

In many businesses, cost of materials is an important part of total cost; sometimes, rising material costs (e.g. when oil prices spike and drag plastic prices up with them) endanger a company's profit model. One solution is to use materials that are junk, discarded and available for free. Here is a good example — the Freitag brothers, in Switzerland, who create high value from old truck tarpaulins.[3]

"In a high-ceilinged factory in Zurich, old truck tarpaulins are being spread out to be cut up and stitched into idiosyncratic, colorful bags. Destined for sale across Switzerland, the rest of Europe and more recently Japan and the U.S., their popularity has spread far beyond the cycle couriers who first appreciated their practical stylishness and ecological appeal."

"People like us for various reasons," says Daniel, at 41 the older brother by a year. "Our buyers tend to be urban types, often working in the creative industries, like advertising or graphics. They like our functional design and appreciate the quality that comes with manufacturing in Switzerland."

"The brothers say Freitags' green credentials are also a crucial factor in its success. As well as the tarpaulins, almost all the materials they use are recycled, while each workspace in the factory has its own bicycle rack. "Customers know we don't advertise or spend money on celebrity endorsements. They recognize and appreciate the honesty of our range," Daniel says."

"Our biggest initial investment was SFr2,300 — our combined savings at the time — for an industrial sewing machine," says "Daniel. Later, the brothers borrowed SFr20,000 from their parents to fund expansion." "Only twice have they resorted to a bank loan: first to finance their landmark store in Zurich, which comprises a stacked pile of freight containers, and more recently to help equip their new factory. There are now nine stores, including outlets in New York and Tokyo. Profits are a carefully guarded secret but revenues this year seem likely to approach SFr30million."

How in the world did they get the idea? Here is how: "Markus was on a course in graphic design. His shared student flat looked over the Zurich flyover that carries much of the transalpine truck traffic. Somehow, seeing all those trucks, and knowing there was a gap in the market, inspiration bloomed."

Innovator! When you see junk — do you see value and creativity? Can you too build a powerful business, like the Freitags, out of junk?

---

[3]Haig Simonian, *Bags of cash from cast-offs*, The Financial Times, January 4, 2012.

Johnny Cash: How his career began in Folsom Prison

Johnny Cash was one of America's greatest country music singers, popular far beyond country fans. His career took off in large part because of a bold risk he took — he appeared before inmates in Folsom Prison, sang the song he wrote about Folsom, and then issued an album based on his live performance. It is regarded as one of the greatest albums ever.

> I hear the train a comin', it's rollin' 'round the bend,
> And I ain't seen the sunshine, Since, I don't know when,
> I'm stuck in Folsom Prison, and time keeps draggin' on,
> But that train keeps a-rollin', on down to San Antone.

According to *Wikipedia*, Cash was inspired to write this song after seeing the movie *Inside the Walls of Folsom Prison* (1951) while serving in West Germany in the United States Air Force. Cash recounted how he came up with the "Reno" line: "I sat with my pen in my hand, trying to think up the worst reason a person could have for killing another person, and that's what came to mind."

> When I was just a baby, My Mama told me, "Son,
> Always be a good boy, don't ever play with guns,"
> But I shot a man in Reno, Just to watch him die,
> When I hear that whistle blowin', I hang my head and cry.

Cash brought along his girlfriend June Carter, also a country singer. Her performance is also on the album. Cash got a great reception; Carter, as one can imagine, got a roof-raising one.

> I bet there's rich folks eatin', in a fancy dining car,
> They're probably drinkin' coffee, and smokin' big cigars,
> But I know I had it comin', I know I can't be free,
> But those people keep a-movin', and that's what tortures me.

What I learn from this episode is this: In a career, the shortest distance between two innovative points is almost never a straight line. In Cash's case, it was a crooked line (literally), that ran through Folsom Prison. Cash had a rapport with the inmates and you can hear it in the album. It showed he was not a spoiled country star but a real person, a working class singer who understood those he sang for and sang about. Innovator: In your career, innovate not just products or services. Innovate your career. Take crooked paths to your destination. Take risks. Go where others don't dare. You won't regret it.

Cash performed at Folsom Prison itself on January 13, 1968 and the *At Folsom Prison* album was released the same year. His career took off, and lasted several decades.

Folsom State Prison is located in the city of Folsom, California. Opened in 1880, it is the second-oldest prison in the state of California after San Quentin. Folsom was one of the first maximum security prisons, and as such hosted the execution of 93 condemned prisoners over a 42-year period.

Reverse innovation revisited: What the poor teach the rich

Business Professor Vijay Govindarajan's new book is about 'reverse innovation' (innovating for the poor, leveraging the result for the rich). Here is an excerpt from an excellent *YouTube* talk by Prof. Govindarajan about this important idea.[4]

"What is reverse innovation? Why is it so important? What is it that multinationals must do to master reverse innovation?

Think about the innovation paradigms inside GE, P&G, Pepsi, IBM, Cisco, Nestle and others. Historically, MNCs design products in rich countries, and sell them in poor ones. Reverse innovation involves the opposite, innovating in poor countries and bringing the products to rich ones.

---

[4]https://youtu.be/ztna1lt_LZE

Clearly poor people want what rich people have. But why would a rich man want a poor man's product? That is the essence of reverse innovation.

* Nestle: is remaking itself as a health and wellness company. The place they are looking to innovate is emerging markets, because of the size of the consumer base. They innovated under the brand name Maggi (noodles), in India, low fat healthy noodles. It created a huge market in India, but is now sold successfully in rich countries.

* Tata Nano: $2,000 car. The cost of a DVD player in a BMW is much more! They target the two-wheeler population in India. Two-wheelers cost $1,500. A $2,000 car will win the two-wheeler population. You are converting non-consumers into consumers. This is fundamental innovation. Tata Motors plans to bring the Nano into Europe and the U.S. This will transform the global auto business.

* GE. Five years ago GE pioneered an ultra low cost portable ultrasound machine in China. It costs $15,000. Contrast that with the premium ultrasound machines, sold for $350,000. Why do you need a portable machine in China? 90 percent of China is rural. You have no hospitals. The hospital has to come to the patient. So the machine must be portable. The low cost portable machine, innovated for China, is now creating markets for GE all over the world, including the U.S. It is a $300 million global business for GE.

In the U.S., you can put the portable ultrasound machine in an ambulance, when there is an accident.

How come reverse innovation has become so important? It is because of the *2008–2009 Great Recession*. It has fundamentally reset the world. Growth has shifted from developed to developing countries, from rich to poor. 15 years ago, GE used to prepare its global strategy, so there was a strategy for the U.S., Europe, Japan and the rest of the world. Today GE has a BRIC strategy, for the Middle East, and — the rest of the world. This is a fundamental change. MNEs have taken the 7 billion people on earth and divided them into 2 billion rich people, and 5 billion poor. The latter were left to government and charity. This is outmoded. We need to bring the 5 billion poor into the consumer base. They cannot consume the same products consumed by the 2 billion rich base. There is no product created for Middle America ($50k per capita) that can be adapted to capture middle India ($800 per capita).

What should the MNEs do to master reverse innovation? (1) Have a big dream for emerging markets. Unless you think big, you won't become big. (2) Make "amplifying weak signals" a core competence. The future is unknowable. There are many "weak signals" in emerging markets, MNEs are unused to hearing them. They must become expert at it. You cannot wait for the weak signal to become clear before you act. By the time the signal is clear, the game is over. The golden rule is, spend a little, and learn a lot. Keep the cost of failure cheap. Then you can fail more often. Failure is converting assumptions into knowledge. Fail early, fail fast, fail cheap. (3) Fundamentally change the center of gravity of your organization. You have to massively redeploy resources from rich lands to poor ones. Delegate power. Localize power and resources in emerging markets. This is hard for MNEs.

John's Phone: Innovation by subtraction

A friend and reader drew my attention to this cell phone innovation. It is called "John's Phone". It isn't cheap; it costs $100, and $150 for the premium (gold) version. It's the world's most basic cell phone. All you can do with it is make calls and receive them. Nothing else. Basic basic. It was designed by the Dutch firm John Doe Amsterdam, and is especially good for kids, or elderly people, or those who HATE technology. It made the top 12 of the *Year's Best Ideas in Interface Designs.*

John's Phone has a sense of humor. John's Phone features a 32-page paper address book kept on the back of the handset. It includes an ink pen that resembles a stylus, a notepad, and a tongue-in-cheek "Games" section (for tic-tac-toe). The designers say that these features allow the phone to be used even when it is turned off. Also included is "text messaging" *which is done in the paper booklet*. The device is not locked, making it compatible with any SIM using the GSM system. The keypad consists of only the numbers 0–9, an asterisk, a hash, and the call and end buttons.

What does John's Phone prove? There is a constant inherent stubborn bias in innovation toward added complexity and additional features. The result is often needlessly complex, unfriendly products and services. The solution? Take a familiar product or service. Strip it down to the most basic elements. What is the core function of the product, the thing most people use it for? Eliminate everything else. Subtraction, not addition, is the most powerful arithmetical operator for innovation. Subtraction will give you user friendly, simple, cost-effective innovations.

Action learning exercise: Take another product that you like. What is its #1 main use? Eliminate everything else. What do you get? How could you market it? How much could you charge?

Rwanda: Literally, back from the dead

The horrendous Rwanda genocide was a mass slaughter that happened in 1994. In 100 days over 500,000 people were killed, according to a *Human Rights Watch* estimate. But some estimates put the death toll at as much as 1 million, or 20 percent of the entire population.

According to *CNN's* Fareed Zakaria, "Most people assumed that Rwanda was broken and, like Somalia, another country wracked by violence, would become a poster child for Africa's failed states. It's now a poster child for success." Much of the credit goes to its President, Paul Kagame. Zakaria notes, "Average incomes have tripled; the health care system is good enough that the *Gates Foundation* cites them as a model, education levels are rising. The government is widely seen as one of the more efficient and honest ones in Africa. *Fortune* magazine published an article recently titled "Why CEOs Love Rwanda"."

Kagame was the leader of the forces that came in and ended the genocide. He has led the country since then and implemented controversial programs to help build stability in the country. Zakaria: "The only way President Kagame could see to make peace was to reintegrate these communities. He came up with a specially crafted solution — using local courts called Gacacas. In each village, the killers stood before their neighbors and confessed, and in turn were offered forgiveness — part court, and part community council. It has made for a fascinating historical experiment that seems to be working."

I know that Kagame is highly controversial. It is said Rwandan military forces have meddled in the Congo. He is said to be undemocratic and repressive. But look at the data, including *IMF* projections for 2013–2017. They show Rwanda's economy (GDP per capita) growing at 5 percent annually, inflation at a moderate 5 percent, with exports leading the growth engine. Rwanda is also, according to the data, able to attract foreign capital.

Rwanda is now one of Africa's great economic success stories. Kagame has created a highly entrepreneurial economy. Tutsis and Hutus live and work together to build their country. Who would have thought this possible in 1994?

How Sharath Jeevan is making a difference to kids in India

"Ninety-five percent of kids in India have access to free government schools within a half-mile of where they live," says Sharath Jeevan, "a distance of 800 meters. The problem is that many of these schools offer poor-quality education. The average Indian fifth grader reads like a second grader in Britain or the U.S. Two-thirds of them can't read a paragraph or do simple fractions."

I've found that a key differentiator between innovators and those who just have ideas is that the former, innovators, act, while the latter, ideators, just gripe.

Jeevan, originally from India, got a superb education abroad, and then worked with a top consultancy and now with *eBay*. Each time he visited Mumbai, his home town, he became upset. Free public education is great. But it has to educate. So here is what he did.[5]*

Schools and Teachers Innovating for Results was officially introduced in Delhi. Backed by funding from the *British Department for International Development* and a number of British charities, STIR has spent the past 15 months researching the most successful "micro-innovations" — small,

---

[5]D. D. Gutten plan, *In India, Making Small Changes on a Large Scale*, Global New York Times, March 3, 2013.

inexpensive, easy-to-implement changes — in classrooms across India. "We visited 300 schools and conducted 600 face-to-face meetings, speaking to over 3,000 teachers," Jeevan said in an interview at the STIR office in London. "Indian teachers are used to thinking of themselves as instruments of a ministry or of government policy," Mr. Jeevan said. "It was the first time many of them had been asked about anything."

"Through innovation, we wanted to get teachers to think of themselves more seriously — as professionals," he said. "The idea is to create a platform to collect the best of these micro-innovations, test them to see if they work, and then take them to scale. There are 1.3 million schools in India, so scale is a huge problem."

Some of the ideas, recounted in STIR materials, will sound familiar to parents in wealthier countries.

• At Majeediya Madarsa-e-Jadeed, a school catering to a predominantly Muslim community in Seelampur, Iram Mumshad, a teacher, noticed that parents, many of whom worked as day laborers, seemed unaware of how to support their children's education. To engage parents, the school started incorporating their feedback on children's behavior at home into school reports, building relationships between teachers and parents, and underlining the importance of parental support.

• At Babul Uloom, a public school in one of the poorest neighborhoods in East Delhi, Sajid Hasan realized that his students started school with fewer learning skills than students from wealthier parts of the city — a gap that seemed to increase with each passing month. So Mr. Hasan, a member of the *Teach for India* program that puts young, highly motivated teachers in some of the country's toughest schools, decided to give his students extra time to catch up by extending the school day for two hours.

"India normally has one of the shortest school days in the world," Mr. Jeevan said. Most schools finish by 1 p.m. The two extra hours, he said, "gives the children more time to learn and also more structure in their lives. It also helps the teachers to focus on the students' current level to help get them to where they need to be."

• Students at the S.R. Capital School in Shahadra struggled with the poetry included in the curriculum, yet they all seemed well versed in the latest Bollywood hits. So Bindu Bhatia, their teacher, fit the words of the texts studied in class to the tune of popular songs, then encouraged the students to perform the poems, making classes more fun and giving students added confidence in approaching potentially daunting material.

STIR is designed to allow innovative teachers to feel like they are part of a network. "Small changes in practice can make a big difference in the classroom," Mr. Jeevan said. "But what matters more in the long term is the change in how teachers think of themselves."

I think STIR can easily be adapted to every country in the world. Let's stimulate innovation at the ground floor, at the level of the classroom teacher. Who can do it better than they?

Green energy for the poor: The Kenya model

Innovation at its best helps the poor, and uses creativity in its business design, not just in technology. Here is an example, by Ngozi Okonjo-Iweala, former Nigerian finance minister and World Bank official, writing in *The International New York Times*. He recounts the *M-KOPA* system in Kenya, Tanzania and Uganda, that brings cheap clean power to families:

"It's called *M-KOPA*. The "M" stands for 'mobile' and 'kopa' means "to borrow". The company's customers make an initial deposit, roughly $30, toward a solar panel, a few ceiling lights and charging outlets for cell phones — a system that would cost about $200. Then they pay the balance owed in installments through a widely-used mobile banking service …. the solar units are cheaper and cleaner than kerosene, the typical lighting source and once they're fully paid for after about a year, *the electricity is completely free.* More than 200,000 homes in Kenya, Uganda and Tanzania use *M-KOPA's* solar system".

That to me is a "wow". The idea should spread to rural India and to rural China, to Myanmar, and throughout Africa. Note how this system combines technology, business innovation (the mobile payment system), and sensitivity to the needs of the poor. Electric power is vital not just for quality of life, but also for education, so that kids can read and do their homework in the evening.

Special congratulations to the *M-KOPA* innovators! They could be candidates for a *Nobel Peace Prize*.

Bernie Sanders is taking the money out of politics

Senator Bernie Sanders is running a long-shot campaign for the Democratic nomination for President. Like all socialists, he has no chance of actually being elected, but very high probability that some of his ideas will be tamed and adopted by his rivals.

In today's *New York Times*, a strong editorial reveals one other huge gift Sanders brings to the table. He is raising money the old-fashioned way — one small gift at a time. The average donation to Sanders' campaign is $31.30. "It would be hard to buy any politician for $31.30", says *The Times*. Americans of ordinary means have given Sanders 400,000 donations and 80 percent of them were less than $200. Now, contrast that with the fact that 400 of America's wealthiest families, writing huge checks, account for half the money raised so far by both parties, Republicans and Democrats. And Trump? As a billionaire, he pays his own bills... and bought his way into the lead.

America's Supreme Court, notes *The Times*, in its recent *Citizens United* decision, "has greatly boosted the buying power of corporate and special interest donors and made a casino frenzy of the (nomination) race". The Koch brothers, billionaires, organized 400 of their wealthy friends to create a super war chest of $889 million for Republican candidates. Jeb Bush raised over $100 million in big-check donations so far. Even Hillary Clinton has raised over $20 million in super-PAC money.

When democracy is bought by the rich, who invariably seek (and get) favors in return from those whom they help elect, it is no longer democracy. So, good for you, Bernie! Tear a strip off the big donors. You bring honesty and sanity to this weird campaign.

Kids' scores rise when they care about other kids & teachers

It's summer vacation time for school kids. A good time to reflect on what they will return to, in September.

In an Israeli weekly, psychiatrist Ron Berger, who specializes in helping children all over the world who suffer from post-trauma stress disorder, recounts an experiment tried at a small school in northern Israel. The school did poorly in national performance tests. Then Berger and colleagues introduced a program, "A call to giving", which focused on two key elements:

- Mindfulness — "intentional, accepting and non-judgmental focus of one's attention on the emotions, thoughts and sensations occurring in the present moment". Simply being aware of one's own feelings and thoughts in the present.
- Compassion — sympathetic pity and concern for the sufferings or misfortunes of others.

The idea? Create strong bonds among the schoolchildren, first by making each of them aware of their own feelings and identity, then developing a caring attitude toward others, include the teacher.

So — what in the world has this to do with test scores?

Well, apparently a lot. The school now scores among the highest, in Israeli schools, in national tests.

Why? The simple answer could be — kids study best when they like the place in which they go to school, like other kids, like the teachers, and find that the teachers like them. Apparently, children do not thrive in an environment where there is intense pressure to achieve high grades, and where each individual essentially is out for themselves, sink or swim, instead of being part of a tight-knit social community that helps one another.

Is this naïve? Innocent? Simple-minded? Perhaps. But at least at once school, it works. It's worth a try.

Living on 26 rupees a day: Lessons learned

My friend Pramod alerted me to an article on the Indian website *The Hindu*, about two young men from wealthy Indian families who decided to see what it is like to live, as poor Indians (on 26 rupees daily, or fifty cents) and as average Indians, on 100 rupees ($2) a day, (75 percent of all Indians live on less).

Tushar, the son of a police officer in Haryana, studied at the University of Pennsylvania and worked for three years as an investment banker in the U.S. and Singapore. The other, Matt, migrated as a teenager to the States with his parents, and studied in MIT. Both decided at different points to return to India, came to share a flat, and became close friends.

Here is what they learned, on 100 rupees daily: *They found soy nuggets a wonder food — affordable and high on proteins, and worked on many recipes. Parle G biscuits again were cheap: 25 paise for 27 calories! They innovated a dessert of fried banana on biscuits. It was their treat each day. Living on Rs. 100 made the circle of their life much smaller. They found that they could not afford to travel by bus more than five kilometers in a day. If they needed to go further, they could only walk. They could afford electricity only five or six hours a day, therefore sparingly used lights and fans. They needed also to charge their mobiles and computers. One Lifebuoy soap cut into two. They passed by shops, gazing at things they could not buy. They could not afford the movies, and hoped they would not fall ill.*

Next, they upped the stakes, and decided to live at the poverty line, 26 rupees daily.

For this, they decided to go to Matt's ancestral village Karucachal in Kerala. They ate parboiled rice, a tuber and banana and drank black tea: a balanced diet was impossible on the Rs. 18 a day which their briefly adopted 'poverty' permitted. They found themselves thinking of food the whole day. They walked long distances, and saved money even on soap to wash their clothes. They could not afford communication, by mobile and Internet. It would have been a disaster if they fell ill. For the two 26-year-olds, the experience of "official poverty" was harrowing.

After their experience, they wrote to their friends: "Wish we could tell you that we are happy to have our "normal" lives back. Wish we could say that our sumptuous celebratory feast two nights ago was as satisfying as we had been hoping for throughout our experiment. It probably was one of the best meals we've ever had, packed with massive amounts of love from our hosts. However, each bite was a sad reminder of the harsh reality that there are 400 million people in our country for whom such a meal will remain a dream for quite some time. That we can move on to our comfortable life, but they remain in the battlefield of survival — a life of tough choices and tall constraints. A life where freedom means little and hunger is plenty..."

What did they learn from this?

"It disturbs us to spend money on most of the things that we now consider excesses. Do we really need that hair product or that branded cologne? Is dining out at expensive restaurants necessary for a happy weekend? At a larger level, do we deserve all the riches we have around us? Is it just plain luck that we were born into circumstances that allowed us to build a life of comfort? What makes the other half any less deserving of many of these material possessions, (which many of us consider essential) or, more importantly, tools for self-development (education) or self-preservation (healthcare)?"

And finally, they learned: "That hunger can make you angry. That a food law which guarantees adequate nutrition to all is essential. That poverty does not allow you to realize even modest dreams. And above all — in Matt's words — that empathy is essential for democracy."

Summing it all up: How our brains innovate

How do our brains cook up creative ideas? Functional MRI imaging now enables scholars to track precisely which areas of the brain are involved, when the brain is trying to be creative. Using this tool, Haifa University researcher Dr. Naama Mayseless (in her doctoral research, directed by Prof. Simone Shamay-Tsoory), Dept. of Psychology, found that:

"…. for a creative idea to be produced, the brain must activate a number of different — and perhaps even contradictory — networks. Developing an original and creative idea requires the simultaneous activation of two completely different networks in the brain: the associative — "spontaneous" — network alongside the more normative — "conservative" — network."

In the first part of the research, respondents were give half a minute to come up with a new, original and unexpected idea for the use of different objects. Answers which were provided infrequently received a high score for originality, while those given frequently received a low score.

In the second part, respondents were asked to give, within half a minute, their best characteristic (and accepted) description of the objects. During the tests, all subjects were scanned using an FMRI device to examine their brain activity while providing the answer.

For the answer to be original, an additional region worked in collaboration with the associative region — the administrative control region. A more "conservative" region related to social norms and rules. The researchers also found that the stronger the connection, i.e. the better these regions work together in parallel — the greater the level of originality of the answer.

"On the one hand, there is surely a need for a region that tosses out innovative ideas, but on the other hand there is also the need for one that will know to evaluate how applicable and reasonable these ideas are. The ability of the brain to operate these two regions in parallel is what results in creativity. It is possible that the most sublime creations of humanity were produced by people who had an especially strong connection between the two regions," the researchers concluded.

In short: An often-repeated theme in this book is confirmed: Innovate with your head in the clouds ("associative brain") and your feet on the ground (administrative pragmatic brain).

I think the crucial connections that Dr. Mayseless discovered can be strengthened. Think of creative ideas. Then think of how to make them practical, useful, feasible, implementable. Together, those two brain centers can change the world.

Now, let's go out and do it.

Epilog

Your PIM — Personal Innovation Machine

"Thinking is more interesting than knowing," Goethe once said, "but less interesting than looking." And, I would add, far less interesting than doing.

Innovation at its best translates creative thought into inspired action. Creativity without action is dreaming — entertaining, enjoyable, but not world-changing. Creativity with action is world-changing innovation.

I hope that readers, after reading these stories, will take action. My recommendation: Build your own PIM — (Personal Innovation Machine). Build your own personal, unique system for ideation — coming up with ideas — along with idea validation, and pragmatic implementation. Make sure it is consistent with your own personality, goals, vision, dreams and nature. Make sure that it fits you, like a tailored dress or suit of clothes.

A good way to do this is to write a story, perhaps like those in this book. What is your story? Look ahead 5 or 10 years. Imagine yourself as you will be. You have come up with a great idea and then transformed it into an innovation that makes a great many people happy. How did you do this? Tell your story, as a way of describing in concrete terms your own PIM (Personal Innovation Machine). What tools did you use? How did you use them? Keep in mind that "machine" implies some sort of system, while creative ideation, head in the clouds, and implies open unbounded thinking. How can you make these two, the wolf of creativity and the lamb of discipline, lie down together?

Which of the 100-plus stories in this book have you found most useful, enlightening and inspiring? How can you apply the tools they embody? Which of the tools suit you best, personally?

"Knowing" is to master existing knowledge. This is necessary, even vital. But we must add to knowing, 'thinking', challenging existing knowledge. This is interesting. To "thinking", we must add "looking" — constantly scanning the world, identifying challenges, problems, and unmet needs, ways we can improve the world and change it. And to "looking", we must add the key ingredient, the "yeast" that makes the dough rise, *doing!*

How will *your* Personal Innovation Machine combine knowing, thinking, looking, doing, to change the world?

Index